# Dragons
## and Fairways

### The Great Welsh Golfers

Richard Clifford

Gomer

Acknowledgements

Thanks to all the golfers included in these chapters for their
time and endless supply of interesting stories and anecdotes.
I would also like to thank the following for their help in the
research and production of this book.

Anthony Woolford, Media Wales Golf Correspondent,
Ceri and all the staff at Gomer, Tony Woolway and
Robert Mager in the Media Wales library, John Jermine
and all at Ryder Cup Wales 2010, The Golf Union of
Wales, The Ladies' European Tour, Peter Alliss and
BBC Sport, East Tennessee State University Athletics
Department... and Amanda and Bethany for all their
support.

Published in 2010 by
Gomer Press, Llandysul, Ceredigion, SA44 4JL

ISBN 978 1 84851 101 9

A CIP record for this title is available from the British Library.

This book is published with the financial support of the
Welsh Books Council.

Printed and bound in Wales at
Gomer Press, Llandysul, Ceredigion

# Contents

Celtic Manor

# Introduction

## WELSH GOLF GETS EVER BETTER
## BY JOHN JERMINE, CHAIRMAN, RYDER CUP WALES 2010

THAT Welsh golf has never been stronger or better placed to bring in new people to the game and introduce them to a lifetime's pleasure is not in question, nor is its ability to keep producing wonderfully talented players.

A country's golfing pedigree is earned, not by accident, but as the result of generations of endeavour and commitment, almost from the time the game began. Would Bernard Darwin, the first literary giant of golf, who learned to play at one of Wales's founding clubs, Aberdovey – whose first nine holes were laid out using the now famous Flower Pots – have been surprised at the emergence of Wales as a powerful golfing nation? I think not, for while he described Aberdovey as the course 'my soul loves best' he recognised the passion of others in Wales for their courses and for golf.

The first Welsh courses were full of quality, including Royal Porthcawl, Conwy and Tenby, and, in 1895, seven of them formed what would become the world's third oldest Golfing Union, with Colonel Ruck, Darwin's uncle, as its first secretary. The last 'amateur' secretary, who gave of his time for the minimum honorarium, was John Treharne, based in the back room at his home in Burry Port, very close to his beloved Ashburnham, but the move to Celtic Manor Resort in 1995, in the centenary year, fittingly marked the beginning of a new era that in 2007 saw the merging of the Men's and Women's Unions designed to make the game in Wales more inclusive and better than ever.

In living memory are many others who helped nurture the game in Wales during the difficult and dark days when I know, from personal experience, how hard the players and teams struggled to achieve the success we all wanted so much.

Our first golfing icon was Dai Rees, three times runner-up at The Open and five times Ryder Cup Captain, including for the famous win at Lindrick, in 1957, the only victory between 1933 and 1985 (when Tony Jacklin inspired Europe to its first victory at The Belfry). From Fontygary, and with a fiery reputation, he built a magnificent platform for Welsh involvement in the Ryder Cup, later cemented by others, especially Brian Huggett, who had a wonderful personal playing record in his six matches and was, in 1977, the last ever captain of the GB&I team; and, of course, Ian Woosnam, four times in a winning team and, in 2006, the charismatic skipper of the victorious Europeans in Ireland.

But others, too, must be remembered. My first golfing hero was Tony Duncan, the 'Colonel', held, by me and all my contemporaries, in awe and with huge respect. As the playing captain of the 1953 GB&I Walker Cup team, he chose not to play himself, recognising 'that I was definitely the weakest in the team' – probably not true but a mark of the man. His golfing home was Southerndown, my first love among the true championship courses, where, in 1959, he hosted for the first time the 'Duncan Putter', a 72-hole event played annually at Easter, in all winds and weathers and with the ubiquitous sheep seeking shelter under the gorse. The Welsh golfers of the day wanted the opportunity to play against the best players from the other home countries, and such was Duncan's stature that he could be sure that few, if any, of the prized invitations, posted every year without fail on January 1, would ever be turned down. Townshend, Oosterhuis, Benka, McEvoy and Wolstenholme are just a few names that give testimony to him and after fifty years the 'Putter' is still one our most prestigious and important tournaments.

In 2008, Andy Morgan, a member of Cardiff and Royal Porthcawl, marked the completion of his two-year term as President of the European Golf Association with a magnificent dinner for the Presidents of Europe's golfing nations, held at the Welsh National Museum and honoured by the presence of the First Minister of Wales, Rhodri Morgan. First elected to the Council of the WGU in 1975, Andy's influence is a theme running through many of the ground-breaking initiatives that produced, through the 1980s and 1990s, outstanding Welsh success, individually and in teams. Structurally too, he has given Wales the international credibility and confidence to successfully bid to host the 2010 Ryder Cup, the biggest event in world golf, and described by our First Minister as 'Wales's Olympics'.

He oversaw the appointment of Craig Defoy as National Coach in 1986, influencing so positively the development and careers of so many great players, Golfing Academies and Squads, the very best teaching professionals and the relocation of the Union to Celtic Manor Resort. He also played a crucial role in galvanizing support throughout golfing Wales for the 2010 Ryder Cup bid that was brilliantly co-ordinated by Tony Lewis, perhaps better known as a former England cricket captain, but with a real love of golf. Tony managed the impossible by getting the whole of Wales to pull together and by securing the complete and essential support of Rhodri Morgan and the Welsh Assembly Government, and Sir Terry Matthews, the owner and driving force behind Celtic Manor. What a team and what a country to produce them all in the same generation – almost as though it was always meant to be!

Our first British Amateur Champion was Duncan Evans, winner at Royal Porthcawl in 1980, succeeded by Philip Parkin, once described by 'Monty' – Europe's

2010 captain Colin Montgomerie – as the most talented American-university player he had seen. Then came Paul Mayo and Stephen Dodd who played at Brynhill Golf Club under the guidance of the doyen of all Junior Organisers, John Collins, the deserved winner in 2005 of the Sir Henry Cotton Award for his services to junior golf.

Equally importantly, Welsh teams have emerged as powerful representatives of a country now respected throughout the world of golf. Since 1993, when Wales won the Men's European Team Championships, our first international team trophy, other trophies have followed: the European Youths Team Championships in 1998 under the captaincy of Tony Disley, long-time custodian of the Union's finances and now the Chairman of the GB&I selectors, and, in 2002, at Wales's other wonderful Royal links course, Royal St David's, Harlech, the Home Internationals, with Andy Ingram at the helm. In 2006, in South Africa, with Jeff Toye, from Radyr, twice Welsh Amateur Champion, as captain. Wales finished fourth in the Eisenhower Trophy, the world amateur team championships – and we are a golfing nation with only 4% of UK golfers and fewer courses than in Surrey!

Amateur success has fed into the professional ranks with Bradley Dredge and Stephen Dodd winning the 2005 World Cup in Portugal, and the two Beckys – Brewerton and Morgan – finishing third in the 2006 World Team Championships, held at Sun City, South Africa. Becky Brewerton's selection as the first ever Welsh player in the 2007 Solheim Trophy team, and again in 2009, was a fantastic achievement bringing great personal honour as well as reflected glory to her club, Abergele, and to Wales. Becky is a wonderful successor to Tegwen Matthews who represented Wales with such vigour and success just a few years earlier and, more recently, captained our women's team with the same enthusiasm and drive.

So why am I confident that we have more and better to come?

Throughout our history we have oozed quality; Royal Porthcawl, my own little square of heaven that could so easily have been Royal St David's had I been born in the north; Radyr, where I started playing golf and a wonderful jewel designed by Harry Colt, a heritage shared with Pyle & Kenfig, and since 2005, Machynys Peninsula, Llanelli, a wonderful Gary Nicklaus championship course where Brian Huggett is the President and the Rev Eldon Phillips is shared with Llanelli Scarlets as honorary chaplain, and is the 'Starter Extraordinaire'! Aberdovey, Conwy and Nefyn, with its spectacular scenery, are more wonderful golfing destinations in the north but there are many others, north and south, that offer an enjoyable and challenging day's golf.

Our golfing routes compare favourably with any throughout the golfing world and Wales is becoming a truly international golfing destination offering the best value for money in Europe. Our golfing visitors have increased by over 50% since Wales won the bid. Our players, captains and administrators have always kept us moving forwards, some times more slowly than others, but, since the late 1970s, punching above our weight, and now, with the 'TwentyTen' course at Celtic Manor Resort, we have our first 'Trophy' course and a flagship to attract the world's golfing legions that is set to become the 'Gateway to Golfing Wales'.

Hosting the Ryder Cup has brought us all together and there is a growing awareness of the huge benefits it is already bringing to Wales. With the support of the European Tour and the PGA, the Sports Council for Wales and, critically, our Welsh Assembly Government, golf has been introduced to over 43,000 children between 11 and 16 years of age and is now established as a Dragon Sport in our primary schools; 41 new pay-and-play facilities across the whole of Wales, that have been funded by the Ryder Cup Wales Legacy Fund, will be opened by 2011. And the Ryder Cup Wales official charity, Tenovus, has already launched the first mobile unit in the world designed to treat cancer patients nearer their homes.

The newly merged Golf Union of Wales representing every golfer in Wales, chaired by Louise Fleet and headed by the Chief Executive for over 20 years, Richard Dixon, has launched a new package of initiatives to attract new talent into the management roles for our teams, with training programmes for potential captains and managers, as well as a new coaching regime designed to help our elite players move to the next level. The Sports Council has helped fund five wonderful new, and truly world-class, Centres of Excellence at Llangefni, Ynys Môn, Clays in Wrexham, the Vale of Glamorgan Hotel, Golf and Spa, Machynys and at Celtic Manor Resort, and they will be wonderful resources for our most talented players and coaches.

Will Becky Brewerton play for the third time in the next Solheim Trophy team and will she be joined by another of our talented youngsters starting to make their mark?

Will Bradley Dredge, currently our highest ranked player, or Rhys Davies, a wonderfully talented and delightful young man from Royal Porthcawl, who recently won his full Tour card for 2010, win places in the Ryder Cup team in October?

I hope so and wish them and all of our golfers the very best of luck – the whole of Wales will be rooting for them.

The characters in this book have been instrumental in laying the foundations for golf in Wales; several of them will be an important part of the future and soon there will be a new generation of players, junior organisers, teachers, volunteers and administrators helping Wales to make the most of this unique opportunity.

The world's best golfers will enjoy and be challenged by the magnificent TwentyTen, and 45,000 spectators every day will be joined by millions of television viewers in over a hundred countries further enhancing our international profile. There will be a legacy for everybody in Wales; Welsh golfers will have facilities to rival those anywhere in the world and golf in Wales will be accessible to all and played by many.

Yes, I really am excited and can hardly wait for October 2010 when the 38th Ryder Cup comes to Wales and we can showcase our beautiful country to the world.

Ian Woosnam with rising Welsh stars Ross McLister and Amy Boulden at Royal Porthcawl in 2009

# Chapter One
# Henry Howell

REGARDED by many as the greatest amateur Wales has ever produced, Henry Howell was most definitely a Technicolor character in a monochrome age.

Howell won a staggering eight Welsh Amateur Championship titles during a 13-year span of dominance from 1920-1932 and represented Wales in 29 Home International Series – little wonder he was dubbed the 'Welsh Bobby Jones' by his contemporaries.

It is a record that has never and almost certainly will never be remotely threatened.

Like the great Welsh professionals who would follow him decades later – Rees, Huggett and Woosnam – Howell was short in stature but anything but in personality. To many of the more staid characters of his era, he was something of a rebellious figure, not averse to the pleasures of smoking, drinking and gambling. Indeed, there was nothing Howell liked more than the odd wager on the outcome of a golf game – which led to a story now legendary among those members who have followed in his footsteps around the Glamorganshire links at Penarth, where Howell became a member at the age of ten and was a permanent fixture for the next 59 years until his retirement.

One of the most prestigious tournaments in the Glamorganshire calendar is the annual Howell Cup, originally presented to the club by Henry's father. To qualify for the Cup, members first had to submit three cards, and one evening in June 1926 Howell, having already put in two, was sat in his usual spot at the bar readying himself to play another 18 holes. At which point the conversation turned to what Howell might score and how long it might take him to complete the round.

His gambler's instinct taking over. Howell thought he could shoot 72 in one-and-a-half hours, and laid odds of 5-1 against it for anyone who was prepared to stand up their money. Soon Howell was being asked to take 6-1 against a score of 70 in 90 minutes, and 10-1 against dipping below 70 in 75 minutes. Howell, being Howell, accepted all bets, including one of 40-1 against an outlandish round of 65 in 70 minutes.

The book closed. Howell stepped onto the first tee accompanied by a marker and a timekeeper, and what followed is surely one of the most remarkable rounds of golf ever played.

He holed out at the 18th just 68 minutes later having taken only 63 strokes – an achievement that earned him a place in the Guinness Book of Records. Ironically, the

13

somewhat non-conformist way in which Howell went about his business probably prevented him from reaching the heights which his talent no doubt deserved.

Howell's domestic dominance should have earned him at least one, if not more, Walker Cup appearances, but the letter from the Great Britain and Ireland selectors never dropped through his door.

Born just before the dawn of a new century on October 23, 1899 in Penarth, Henry Rupert (HR) Howell always wanted to stand out from the crowd. From the moment he first showed a talent for golf, Howell cut a dashing figure around the fairways and greens of South Wales. His trademark moustache and sculpted hair were always accompanied by an immaculate outfit – two immaculate outfits if he was playing 36 holes in one day – and rarely was Howell seen without his Crown and Anchor Board which allowed him to indulge in his other great love, gambling.

Given his small frame Howell was never the longest of hitters, but an unerring accuracy off the tee and a short game that was head and shoulders above most of his rivals, were the keys to his success.

His maiden success in the Welsh Amateur was at Southerndown in 1920 – the first staging of the event since 1913 and the ensuing Great War – when he defeated John Duncan at the last hole in the final. He added three more in successive years from 1922 to 1924, and then four in succession from 1929 to 1932. In 1927 he was signed up by the Western Mail to write an exclusive column, one that was particularly well received, and which proved that not only did Howell talk and play a great game, he also wrote a great game too!

He led Glamorganshire to more than a dozen successes in the Welsh Team Championship and Victory Shield Foursomes, and was the leading light in the 'Erratics' Golf Society, made up of the most prominent amateur players in South Wales of the time.

At St Andrews in 1930, Howell reached the quarter-finals of the Amateur Championship, won that year by the legendary American Jones, but arguably his finest hour came at Royal Troon in the 1932 Home International Series – the first of its kind involving the four home nations.

As champion of Wales, Howell took his position at the top of the playing order and proceeded to defeat the Irish champion, John Burke, the English title holder, Eric Fiddian and the Scottish number one, Eric McRuvie – preferred in that position to the reigning Scottish champion Jack McLean – all by the same 2&1 margin. His three victories – along with young McLean – were all included in the 1932 Great Britain and Ireland Walker Cup team comprehensively beaten by the United States at Brookline, Massachusetts, but Howell was, almost inexplicably, overlooked. *Golf Illustrated*, the most influential publication of the day, devoted an editorial to the controversial non-selection of the Welshman, but it did little to change the minds of those who handed out the GB&I blazer badges.

Howell, although not in the same rich vein of form, was still seen as a genuine contender for the 1934 team which was soundly thrashed by the same 9½-2½ margin as two years previously, this time over the Royal St George's Links at Sandwich. Again the call never came, amid rumours that Howell's perceived vices and penchant for all things fashionable marked him down as something of a loose cannon among the Oxbridge-dominated Walker Cup set.

Howell might have thought the wrongs would be righted a couple of years later when he received a letter from the Royal and Ancient inquiring as to his availability, if selected, to join a GB&I team travelling to play in Australia. Howell responded by indicating his availability and desire to play, only to receive a return letter informing him the team had been chosen and his services were surplus to requirements.

Since he had led Wales with distinction, there was a strong lobby for Howell to be named as GB&I's non-playing captain for the 1938 Walker Cup matches at St Andrews. Rather predictably, however, the Walker Cup selection panel, without a Welshman among them, ignored Howell's claims and opted instead for Englishman John Beck. Whether by luck or judgement their selection was vindicated as Beck presided over GB&I's first success over the Americans in the series.

Howell's standing in domestic golf remained undiminished as he continued to represent Wales as he approached his fifties.

He became the secretary at his beloved Glamorganshire club in the early 1960s and then moved to Rhodesia where he spent ten years before returning to South Wales.

Howell lived out his final years in retirement in Worthing, Sussex before his death at the age of 83 in the summer of 1983.

Today his flamboyance would undoubtedly have been a major asset, rather than a hindrance which it proved to be for a man who was, in many ways, ahead of his time.

The stylish Howell in his plus fours with fellow members of the Glamorganshire club at Penarth in 1932
*(Media Wales)*

15

# Chapter Two
# Dai Rees

WALES's first golfing superstar may have been small in stature but he was very much a sporting giant.

Does that sound suspiciously like Ian Woosnam? Think again, because a generation before Woosie arrived on the scene, 'Little' Dai Rees was captivating galleries around the world. Indeed, Rees was one of the first truly global players and his contribution to the development of the professional game cannot be overstated, his name being indelibly etched into Open Championship and Ryder Cup history.

Peter Alliss, the voice of BBC television golf and a great friend and contemporary of Rees, describes him as, 'one of the truly great Britons.'

'Dai was a Welshman first and foremost, and very proud of his homeland, but he was never one to get involved in the politics of devolution or the separatist movements that became so fashionable at the time,' said Alliss. 'He was a great Welshman but also a great Briton who believed in the notion that together we were stronger.'

Born in Fontygary, Rhoose, in 1913, David James Rees was always destined to become a golfer, his father D.J. Rees himself a professional, first at the Barry Leys club, then at nearby Brynhill before a 25-year stint at Aberdare. The story goes that Rees junior was watching the club champion practising his putting at Barry when, at just five years of age, he was asked if he wanted a go. To the amazement of everyone he took the putter and holed out.

It was at Aberdare that Rees junior began to build on his genuine promise and he became an assistant pro at the club before being appointed match professional at Whitchurch, where his payment of £125 a year raised some eyebrows among the more frugal, and conservative, club members. But Rees was soon displaying the sort of competitive instinct that would become as much of a trademark as his simple, smooth, golf swing and his dapper dress sense.

Rees never lacked confidence and there are those who recall his bold claim that he was 'off to show the other assistants how to play' when embarking on his bid to win the PGA Assistants' title in 1934. He finished runner-up that year before winning the title in 1935 and defending it successfully in 1936.

Rees left Wales to take up a position at Surbiton Golf Club, although he remained fiercely proud of his heritage, always displaying a Welsh Dragon on his tournament bag.

The onset of World War II was to disrupt, and in many cases end, many a

Dai Rees in full swing

Dai Rees, right, with Pilot
Officer Monty Griffiths next to a
shot down German plane
*(Media Wales)*

promising sporting career, and Rees went off to serve his country in the Royal Air
Force.

Rees drove motor transport in the RAF and his fellow servicemen were aware
of his sporting prowess even in the heat, humidity and tension of the Middle East
during the war years. In a letter to The Western Mail in 1941, Pilot-Officer M. J.
Griffiths of Newport wrote:

Dai Rees, the golfer, is out here. He gets an occasional game and his form is truly
amazing considering his lack of practice. He was round the Gezira course in Cairo
in 65 the other day. The course record is 67.

After the war Rees returned to Britain and a position at Hindhead golf club,
before succeeding the legendary Harry Vardon at South Herts in 1946, where he
was to remain ensconced as the club professional for a remarkable 37 years until his
death in 1983.

His loyalty and dedication to the club were unquestionable, but it was in the
ever-expanding tournament arena that Rees really shone, as his list of tournament
successes testifies, and which includes four British PGA Matchplay titles in 1936,
'38, '54 and '61, the Dunlop Masters, the DAKS, the Spaldings and the PGA closed
championship. He won Open championships in Switzerland, Egypt and Belgium
and in all he claimed a remarkable 39 career tournament wins.

But it is with the Ryder Cup and the British Open Championship that Rees's
name would always be linked.

His first Ryder Cup appearance came as a 24-year-old in 1937, and he would
eventually be involved in nine series, five of those as captain, and only the war,
resulting in the cancellation of the 1939 matches, stopped him from reaching double
figures. His collective seven wins and one half from 17 foursomes and singles was
a record that stood head and shoulders above most of his Great Britain and Ireland

contemporaries during an era when the USA enjoyed almost complete dominance of the event.

At Lindrick in 1957 Rees enjoyed arguably his finest hour, leading GB&I to victory by 7½-4½, and that after they had lost the foursomes 3-1, Rees and Ken Bousfield providing the only point for the home side. There was controversy when, after Rees's team meeting, Max Faulkner and Harry Weetman apparently 'volunteered' to stand down from the afternoon singles, an incident that led Weetman to proclaim that he would never again be involved in a Ryder Cup as long as Rees was captain. Incidentally, he did appear again under his captaincy in 1959.

Controversy or not, Rees's captaincy style was vindicated as GB&I won six and halved one of the eight singles, the Welshman himself defeating Eric Furgol 7&6. And the Americans, who had been expecting a comfortable win over a course that suited them far more than the traditional British links, did not take too kindly to the defeat. In fact, it was to be GB&I's only victory in the matches between 1933 and 1985, when the format was revised to see a European team replacing the British Isles.

'Dai was perfectly suited to team golf because his enthusiasm was so infectious,' said Alliss, a fellow member of the victorious class of '57. 'He could be an inspirational man and that marked him out as a great captain. 1957 was the pinnacle and perhaps he was encouraged to continue as captain for a shade too long after that, but who could blame people for asking, or Dai for accepting?'

That triumph at Lindrick heightened Rees's profile to hitherto unheard of levels. He was named Golfer of the Year and BBC Sports Personality of the Year. To this day he remains the only golfer to have won that award.

Winning captain Rees is lifted into the air after the 1957 Ryder Cup victory over the USA at Lindrick

*(Media Wales)*

In 1958 he was awarded the CBE from Queen Elizabeth II and later that year he was asked to play alongside Belgium's King Baudouin in a pro-am event at Gleneagles.

Rees, according to Alliss, was a man who lived life to the full and had few regrets, but one of those was his failure to etch his name onto the famous Open Championship Claret Jug.

He came close, closer than any Welshman with the exception of Dave Thomas.

In 1946 at St Andrews, Rees finished fourth and at Troon in 1950 he was third. It seemed only a matter of when, and not if, he would take golf's greatest prize.

At Carnoustie in 1953 he moved up the leaderboard again, finishing second behind the great American Ben Hogan, and 12 months later it was Australian Peter Thomson who denied him, claiming the first of his five Open titles at Birkdale as Rees, C.H. Scott and Bobby Locke tied for second.

Back at Birkdale in 1961, Rees, now 48, again came within a whisker of a place in one of golf's most exclusive clubs, but again fate was to dictate otherwise. In horrendous conditions on the final day, Rees, after a disastrous seven at the opening hole, played some of the finest golf of his career, but a 3, 4, 3, 3 finish was not quite good enough as the great Arnold Palmer prevailed by a single shot.

'Dai had some opportunities to win the Open and most players never even get that close,' said Alliss. 'He was beaten by some of the great names of the sport and there was no shame in that. I'm sure Dai reflected on those near misses in later years but he was no less of a great player because of them.'

Rees actually entered the Open every year it was played, bar one, from his first appearance at Sandwich in 1932 until a serious bowel illness in 1982 forced him to miss the qualifying event for Troon. The small matter of his daughter's wedding day in 1968 was the only time he didn't participate.

Typically, Rees's response to missing the 1982 event was: 'If I feel well in 12 months' time I will be trying again.'

Sadly he didn't get the chance. In November 1983 he died, aged 70, having been in hospital for seven weeks following injuries sustained in a car crash while travelling home from watching his beloved Arsenal FC.

Welsh golf had lost arguably its greatest son and the pain was felt worldwide. Rees had thought nothing of traveling 30,000 miles to play in Australia, New Zealand, the Far East and the United States. His philosophy was a simple one. He believed he was lucky to be making a living from doing something that he loved, and to nurture the game in far-flung corners of the globe was a pleasure rather than a chore.

Rees always considered himself a beneficiary of the game, and as such he always went out of his way to put back more than he took out. He served the PGA as captain, served his country Wales in numerous World Cups, and served all the clubs to which he was attached, and the many more to which he was afforded honorary memberships, with nothing less than total commitment.

'I will never forget Dai's sheer enthusiasm for the sport,' said Alliss. 'He would drive from one end of the country to the other to take part in a charity event. He spent many hours behind the wheel of his car, and outside his golf and his family, cars and Arsenal FC were his passions.

'I always remember him striking a sponsorship deal with Jaguar and he took great delight in showing off the latest models whenever they came off the production line.

'When he died, golf lost one of its great characters, and I lost a dear, dear friend. Even if you allow for the huge advances in the sport in terms of the players' conditioning and the new equipment, Dai Rees would have been a superstar in any era.'

When Woosnam was named Ryder Cup captain for Europe in 2006, the parallels with Rees were inevitably drawn, and Woosnam, born the year after Rees led GB&I to their historic win at Lindrick, took such comparisons as a huge compliment. Ironically it was in 1991, the year that Woosnam recorded his greatest triumph in the US Masters at Augusta, that Rees became the first Welsh golfer to be inducted into the Welsh Sports Hall of Fame. He now sits up there alongside other true greats such as Gareth Edwards, John Charles and 'Peerless' Jim Driscoll. Exalted company, but no less than Rees deserves.

Those whose memories go back far enough remember him with nothing less than admiration and affection. And if any of Wales's current generation of professionals can achieve anything approaching what 'Little Dai' did, they should be more than happy.

'They don't make too many like Dai Rees today,' contemplated Alliss. 'There have been a lot of very good golfers made in Wales, but not too many better than he.'

A veteran Rees playing in the 1978 Welsh PGA Championship at Whitchurch

*(Media Wales)*

21

Tony Duncan

# Chapter Three

# Lt Col. A.A. Duncan

CHAMPION golfer, talented cricketer and rugby player, army officer and war hero.

It sounds like something from a 'Boy's Own' annual but is, in fact, a real-life description of a true legend of Welsh golf, A.A. Duncan.

In these days where talented youngsters are groomed for success in one sporting discipline from an early age, Anthony Arthur Duncan provides a reminder of a golden age of all-rounders. Golf, of course, became his primary sport, and this was hardly surprising, given the dynasty he was born into.

His father, John Duncan, won Welsh Championship titles at Conwy in 1905 and Rhyl in 1909, and his mother, Margery, was three times the Welsh Ladies' champion. His aunt Blanche was Welsh champion five times and in 1909 John, the managing director of a newspaper publishing company, and Blanche became the only brother and sister to win Welsh titles in the same season. John Duncan, who first played out of the Glamorganshire club at Penarth, went on to become chairman of the Welsh Golfing Union and was one of the founders of the Southerndown club, with whom the family became inextricably linked.

Anthony, who became widely known as just 'Tony' among his friends and colleagues, was born in Cardiff in 1914. Having been produced by such pedigree golfing stock, Duncan first made his mark in 1932 when he won the junior club championship titles at Radyr and Glamorganshire and also took the prestigious junior open medal at Swansea Bay.

Graham Emery, a Welsh sports correspondent of the time, was struck by the talent and maturity of the 18-year-old prospect:

> Mr Anthony Duncan has acquired a lot of experience in competitive golf even though he is only eighteen years of age, and he played with a steadiness and ability that would be the envy of most of us. He is possessed of a fine, compact swing, and is obviously a boy with a big future in golf.

During his education at the famous Rugby School in Warwickshire, Duncan excelled at sport, once featuring in a record-breaking cricketing achievement at Lord's.

Playing against Marlborough, Duncan featured in century opening stands in both innings with his partner D. E. C. Steel, who would go on to become Sir David Steel, the chairman of British Petroleum. From there he won a place at Balliol College, Oxford, (switching from mathematics to history at the end of his first year) and aside

23

from his obvious talent on the golf course, his cricket prowess was again evident as he retired after an undefeated century in the 1934 freshman's match.

That same year Duncan won the first of three successive golf 'Blues' in the Varsity golf match against Cambridge and impressed to such an extent that he was made honorary secretary of the club for the following year, an honour that had never been bestowed on a freshman up to that point.

By the time he enrolled at Oxford, Duncan had already played in a Welsh Championship final, beaten by J.L. Black at Royal Porthcawl. And it was to Porthcawl that he returned in 1934 to represent Wales in the Home Internationals, and achieved yet another first. No Welshman before him had gone through the three days of competition unbeaten. Duncan won three and halved three of his matches.

On leaving Oxford he joined the Welsh Guards to start what would become a distinguished military and sporting career. In 1937 he won the first of his Army golf titles at Princes' in Kent, and successfully defended it the following year at East Lothian. There were also regular appearances in the Army's rugby XV.

As Major A.A. Duncan, he returned to Wales in the summer of 1938 to emulate his father by becoming Welsh Amateur champion. He defeated Prestatyn's Sam Roberts 2&1 in the final at Rhyl for the first of four Welsh titles, and who knows how many more Duncan would have added to that tally had the outbreak of World War Two not caused a seven-year suspension of the event. In 1939, however, he did reach the final of the British Amateur Championship at Hoylake, losing to Alex Kyle in the last pre-war championship.

Duncan's military duties then took over and he was part of the Welsh Guards effort in the liberation of Belgium from the Germans in 1944. The Welsh were the first Allied soldiers into Brussels and many were honoured. Duncan himself was made a Chevalier of the Order of Leopold II and was given the Belgian Croix de Guerre with Palm in 1946.

The resumption of his golf career in 1946 saw Duncan win the Worplesdon Foursomes in partnership with Jacqueline Gordon. Their vanquished opponents in the final were Henry Longhurst, who would become one of the sport's most distinguished writers and broadcasters, and Joan Pemberton. Duncan and Gordon successfully retained their title the following year.

His impressive form continued in 1948 with a second Welsh title, ten years and a World War after the first. Remarkably the final at Porthcawl was an exact repeat of 1938 with Duncan defeating Sam Roberts by the same 2&1 margin. A third Army title over the Royal St George's links at Sandwich, along with a victory in the Oxford and Cambridge Society's President's Putter at Rye, ensured that another shelf would be required in the Duncan trophy cabinet.

He married Ann Patricia Krabbe in 1950 and his Army duties took him to the staff college at Camberley where he became an instructor and a Lieutenant Colonel. But these extra responsibilities seemed not to affect his form on the golf course as his third Welsh title arrived at Ashburnham in 1952 when he stopped John Llewellyn Morgan from completing a third successive championship win. A fourth Army title at Sunningdale was another highlight of the year (three more would follow before his retirement) and the R&A invited him to become captain of the GB&I Walker Cup team for the matches at the Kittansett Club, Cape Cod, Massachussets, in 1953.

He was the first Welshman to captain a Walker Cup team and the only playing captain – although he didn't actually hit a ball in the matches!

Then 39, Duncan chose to leave himself out of the opening day's foursomes matches and watched his team fall 3-1 behind with only Gerald Micklem, the English champion, and John Llewellyn Morgan, the other Welshman in the team, registering a point. And the following day, for the singles, he did the same again, watching from the sidelines as only Morgan and Ronald White managed victories for GB&I in a 9-3 overall defeat.

Asked years later why he hadn't played himself in either series, Duncan simply replied: 'It was obvious that given all the other responsibilities I had to carry out, I was the worst player among the team and that is why I didn't select myself.'

Duncan's sportsmanship never manifested itself so clearly as in that contest when, on the opening day, American Jimmy Jackson was found to have 16 clubs in his bag following an oversight. The penalty for such a breach of the rules would have been immediate disqualification but Duncan insisted that he was not interested in winning the point by default. As such the penalty was modified to the loss of

Duncan driving during his match against England in the 1954 Home Internationals at Royal Porthcawl

*(Media Wales)*

two holes and the players moved on, prompting an inspired headline in the local paper the following day: 'Britannia Waives the Rules.'

Duncan was never afraid to take bold, and at times, controversial decisions, as the great Jack Nicklaus was to find out years later.

Nicklaus and Gary Player contested the final of the 1966 Picadilly World Matchplay Championship at Wentworth, and the referee was one Lt. Col. A.A. Duncan.

At the ninth hole the 26-year-old 'Golden Bear' pulled his drive into a ditch and was forced to take a penalty drop. Then he claimed that an advertisement hoarding was stood between his ball and the green and so claimed another drop, this time without penalty.

Duncan politely, but firmly, refused Nicklaus's request for relief under the 'line of sight' rule and the American, in full voice, dismissed it as 'a bum decision.'

After what was described as a 'warm' exchange of views, Duncan offered to step down as match referee and Gerald Micklem took over for the remainder of the final, which Player won by an emphatic 6&4 margin.

'Between the morning and afternoon rounds in the dressing room Colonel Duncan came along and made his peace with Nicklaus,' reflected Player afterwards. 'It was very dignified of him and I know they ended the exchange with a firm handshake and no hard feelings.'

No hard feelings that was, until a few weeks later when a letter from Nicklaus – which was also sent to various sections of the press – arrived at Duncan's home, with the American once again claiming he had been on the wrong end of a bad decision. Duncan's polite reply reminded Nicklaus of the facts of the incident as he had seen it, with a counter threat to make its contents available to the press. That constituted a line under the episode and the pair never crossed paths again.

He may not have appeared in the Walker Cup in 1953, but Duncan's clubs did see some action in the US Amateur Championship at Oklahoma City a few weeks later. However, his challenge ended early as he exited the tournament at the hands of Hillman Robbins.

His fourth and final Welsh title came in 1954 at Tenby, where he was later made an honorary life member, when he comprehensively defeated Keith Thomas, of Borth and Ynyslas, 6&5. That was 21 years after his first appearance in the final, a longevity that has rarely been equalled. And just as there was a ten-year gap between his first and second Welsh titles, so there was between his President's Putter wins, the latter coming in 1958, by which time his Welsh international career had ended.

He played in the Home Internationals 15 times for his country, was captain on two occasions and, rekindling memories of the Walker Cup in 1953, he took the decision to drop himself from the 1955 team. He actually played 51 times in a Welsh jersey and rarely did his standards drop.

After his retirement from competitive golf, Duncan remained an active participant in the sport as an administrator, becoming chairman of both the Welsh and Walker Cup selection committees, and a member of the R&A. In 1959's New Year's Honours list, he was awarded an OBE for his services to the sport.

He was also architect of the tournament which bears the family name. Looking for a suitable tribute to the memory of his father John, Duncan also wanted to bring the top amateur players from the British Isles to the Southerndown links. As a result, the Duncan Putter was first played in 1959. Since then it has become one of the key early-season strokeplay events on the calendar, now counting towards the Welsh amateur order of merit and being recognised by the GB&I selectors as a guide to possible Walker Cup and St Andrews Trophy hopefuls. The likes of Iestyn Tucker, Peter McEvoy, Paul Way, Gary Wolstenholme, Phillip Price, Bradley Dredge and Nigel Edwards have all won the event, and other distinguished players to have participated include Ian Woosnam, Sandy Lyle, Lee Westwood and Justin Rose. President of the club, Duncan took great pride in seeing the event go from strength to strength although in his later years he was unable to attend due to ill health. He was, however, always kept fully informed of proceedings at his beloved Southerndown.

In January 1998, at the age of 84, he died peacefully at his home in Surrey, where he had lived for several years and was the church warden at St John's, Churt.

One of the great characters of the sport, Duncan was an extraordinary man. He will never be forgotten and the Duncan Putter, now beyond its 50th anniversary, provides a fitting tribute to him, and to his remarkable family.

Charlie Whitcombe, a professional who was beaten by the young Duncan during his spell at Oxford, witnessed at first hand the special qualities that champions exhibit:

'The secret of whatever success young Duncan has obtained lies in his unbounded confidence in himself and in his ability to play golf.'

That probably summed him up perfectly. Whatever he undertook, in the sporting arena or in any other area of life, Duncan was determined to do it properly and with full commitment, or not at all.

There are few golfers who can claim to have played at the top level over three different decades. There was only one Tony Duncan.

## Chapter Four
# Dave Thomas

NO Welshman has managed to get his hands on the famous Claret Jug in the 150-year history of the Open Championship. No Welshman has come closer to doing so than Dave Thomas.

Few can forget the infamous fifteenth-club incident which ultimately cost Ian Woosnam the chance of laying that Welsh bogey to rest at Royal Lytham and St Annes in 2001. But it was at the same venue 43 years earlier in 1958 that a powerfully built 23-year-old, who would go on to become one of the world's foremost course designers, was involved in a dramatic head-to-head with one of the championship's greatest players, Peter Thomson.

At the age of 28, the Australian already had three Open Championships in his locker when he went into a 36-hole play-off against the emerging Thomas, considered by many to be the biggest hitter in the British game at the time. The pair had finished a dramatic 72-holes tied on 278, a record low aggregate for the championship.

But that only scratches the surface of the story. For much of the final round Thomas and Thomson traded blows like two heavyweight title contenders – and at 6ft 2in and tipping the scale at almost sixteen stone, Thomas could have been just that.

They arrived at the 18th on level terms and both hit their drives safely onto the fairway. Thomson put his second ten feet beyond the pin while Thomas came up some fifteen yards short, leaving him with a long two-putt for a par. The 15,000 crowd gasped as the young Welshman shaved the edge of the cup with a bold putt, before seeing his ball come to rest just eighteen inches past. That left Thomson with a putt for birdie to win the title, but his effort lipped out and, in turn, heaped the pressure back on Thomas, who now had to hole his return to force a tie.

'It was a terrifying moment,' he recalled. 'It was the ultimate pressure putt. I couldn't win the Open with it, but I could lose it. Thankfully it went in and then we had to wait to see how Christy O'Connor and Leopoldo Ruiz did in the last pairing.'

Having looked out of contention a few holes earlier, O'Connor and Ruiz both hauled themselves back into the frame and stood on the 18th requiring a par to join Thomson and Thomas in a play-off, or a birdie to better them.

An afternoon of high drama had another twist as both put their drives into sand, O'Connor finishing with a bogey five and Ruiz with a triple-bogey seven.

There were no immediate four-hole play-offs in those days, so Thomas and Thomson had to return the following morning to battle it out over another gruelling 36 holes

Thomas playing in the Dunlop Masters at Royal Porthcawl in 1961

*(Media Wales)*

in the first play-off since South African Bobby Locke had beaten Irishman Harry Bradshaw at Royal St George's, Sandwich, in 1949.

Thomson, who had never finished outside the top two in the championship between 1952 and 1958, set off like a greyhound from the traps the next day and was three strokes ahead of Thomas by the turn, an advantage that he would not relinquish.

Thomas battled back to be one behind after the first 18 and actually drew level two holes into the afternoon round.

However, Thomson's pedigree showed as he went ahead again at the 26th and extended his lead to three shots when Thomas took a five to his three, two holes later. By the final hole Thomson was five shots ahead and could afford the luxury of a bogey and still claim his fourth Open.

Years later, when he was inducted into the World Golf Hall of Fame, Thomson recalled his battle with Thomas saying: 'I couldn't shake Dave off during the final round of regulation play and it didn't get any easier in the play-off. I'd get ahead but he would come charging back at me. That was the real thrill of golf for me. I always thrived in that situation.'

At Muirfield in 1966 Thomas again went desperately close, on this occasion finishing tied second with Doug Sanders, one stroke behind a certain Jack Nicklaus, who claimed the first of his three Open wins. Nicklaus was the only one of the three to birdie the par-five 17th, and that proved to be all that separated them. But, as Thomas later admitted:

'I suppose I had my chances but you can't have too many regrets. Thomson won five Opens and Nicklaus three so if you are going to finish second then it might as well be to that calibre of player.'

The performance at Muirfield saw Thomas become the first recipient of the Braid Taylor Memorial medal, since awarded annually to the GB&I player finishing in the highest position at the Open.

Thomas's road to the Open Championship began in August 1934 when he was born in Newcastle, the son of a mining engineer from Mountain Ash. His formative years were at the Newcastle Gosforth club, where he played much of his golf with Alan Thirlwell, who enjoyed a distinguished amateur career, wining the English Championship and playing in the Great Britain and Ireland Walker Cup side.

Thomas became an assistant professional to Ken Geddes at Gosforth at the age of just fifteen, before moving to the Moortown club in Leeds.

With his powerful build he quickly forged a reputation as one of the longest and straightest hitters in the British game, proving his credentials when he defeated Jimmy Hitchcock in a play-off at Hartsbourne to win the 1955 PGA Assistants' title.

The same year he began to make an impact on the wider stage, claiming the Belgian Open title.

In late 1957, just after he had returned from partnering Dai Rees to third place – finishing tied second in the individual standings – in the Canada Cup, Thomas became the full professional at Sudbury in Middlesex, succeeding the veteran Percy Newbery.

That Canada Cup was one of nine in which Thomas featured (there were also two World Cup appearances), his partnerships with Rees and then Brian Huggett becoming a cornerstone of the Welsh game.

In 1958, the year of his play-off defeat to Thomson, Thomas captured the Dutch Open title before embarking on a globetrotting experience that was to have a major impact on his career. Thomson had invited Thomas to join him for a round-the-world tour, stopping off in New Zealand, Australia, Mexico for the Canada Cup and eventually back to Australia to join his wife Robin.

He returned to Europe the following spring with his reputation greatly enhanced and added the French Open title on his way to securing a Ryder Cup place for the first time. His Ryder Cup debut for GB&I against the United States at the Eldorado club in Indian Wells, California, was notable for the fact that Wales – with Dai Rees as playing captain – had two representatives in the team for the first time. Also included was Peter Alliss, who became a great friend and eventually business partner to Thomas.

Thomas and Harry Weetman managed a creditable half in their foursomes against the great Sam Snead and Cary Middlecoff, but the 25-year-old Welshman was no match for Snead – 22 years his senior – in the singles, going down 6&5 as GB&I were beaten 8½-3½.

The following summer Thomas decided to resign from his post at Sudbury to become a full-time tournament player. He linked up with the Sunningdale club and set his sights on emulating the achievements of the world's best:

'I was staking my future on a five-year gamble. At the time I felt there was no way I could combine the jobs of a club professional and a tournament player. I was doing my own game no good and Sudbury no good. The likes of Thomson, Gary Player, Arnold Palmer and Nicklaus didn't have to worry about what was going on back at the club, and I felt I needed to be in the same position to have a chance to reach my potential.'

There is little doubt that over the next five or six years he did, indeed, establish himself as one of the finest players in Britain.

He won the Esso Golden Tournament three times, in 1961 after a tie with his old adversary Thomson, in 1962 and 1966. There was also a British PGA Matchplay

Thomas, left, with Dai Rees, centre, during an exhibition match at Llanwern golf club in 1965

*(Media Wales)*

title success in 1963, the Olgiata Trophy in Rome the same year, the Silentnight Tournament in 1965 and the Penfold-Swallow and the Jeyes Pro-Am a year later. He even joined forces with his old pal Thirlwell to twice win the Amateur-Professional Foursomes at Wentworth. That famous sporting year of 1966 was arguably Thomas's best and by then he was attached to the Dunham Forest club in Cheshire as touring professional.

Though Thomas had failed to make the Ryder Cup team in 1961 at Royal Lytham, he played in the next three. At East Lake, Atlanta, in 1963, GB&I were humbled 23-9 by Palmer's American side, Thomas failing to win any of his matches but gaining a half against Billy Casper in the first of the singles series. At Royal Birkdale in 1965, Thomas and the Scot, George Will, were involved in two remarkable foursomes matches on the opening day, first sweeping past Palmer and Dave Marr 6&5 before losing by exactly the same margin to the same pair in the afternoon.

The Americans went on to win 19½-12½ and prevailed 23½-8½ at the Champions Club in Houston in 1967, which turned out to be Thomas's final Ryder Cup appearance.

Thomas and Tony Jacklin won both their foursomes on the opening day and secured another half in the fourballs. Thomas brought the curtain down on his GB&I career by sharing the honours with Gene Littler in the singles.

It was often said that had Thomas possessed a short game to match his remarkable accuracy and distance off the tee – he once drove the green at Royal Liverpool's 420-yard second hole – then he would have been a regular contender in the Majors. He was also hampered during the early 1960s by a troublesome back problem. His playing career continued into the early 1970s but by then Thomas was already forging a golfing reputation without a club in his hand.

Dave Thomas Ltd had been established as far back as 1958 to promote his golf and commercial activities as a player, but after his tournament career came to an end the golf-course design business began to flourish. Thomas and Alliss were to work together on 80 different projects before going their separate ways, Alliss's broadcasting commitments taking up more and more of his time.

Their most famous venture was undoubtedly The Belfry, which has staged four of the most dramatic Ryder Cups in history. The pair turned a flat and relatively featureless piece of grazing farmland and potato fields in the Midlands into one of the most recognisable courses in the world. The Brabazon course staged Europe's 1985 triumph, the 14-14 tie four years later, America's win under Tom Watson in 1993 and the unforgettable success for Sam Torrance's Europe in 2002.

Thomas recalls his first reaction in 1973 to the landscape that would go on to produce so much drama and inspire so many cheers and tears:

'It was pretty flat and pretty bland and the only thing that got me really excited was the water. We had the brook to work with and we dug out the landscape to make the water the feature of the course it is today.'

Thomas tweaked the course again in 1999 and was one of the proudest men in golf when the course which he built hosted the 2002 Ryder Cup during his own tenure as captain of the PGA. He had been made an honorary member of the PGA in 1994 and served as captain in 2001 – the Association's centenary year – and 2002.

'To be asked to captain the PGA is one of the greatest honours in our profession.

But to be captain in the centenary and to see a Ryder Cup played on the course you designed is just the ultimate way to top off a wonderful career in the game.'

Thomas went on to design the PGA National course at The Belfry and undertook a redesign of the Turnberry links. Among his other high profile designs are Slaley Hall, La Manga and San Roque.

These days the chances are anywhere you go in the world you will not be too far from a Dave Thomas Ltd project. They have built courses in such far-flung corners of the globe as China, Belarus, the Ukraine, Nigeria and the Ivory Coast. Thomas's son, Paul, himself a former European Tour player, is now managing director of the company and has taken over the mantle from his father, who lives in Spain but has maintained a consultancy role.

Thomas was inducted into the Welsh Sports Hall of Fame in 2002, the third golfer to be honoured following Dai Rees and Vicki Thomas.

More than half a century has passed since his heroics at Royal Lytham and who knows for how much longer Dave Thomas can lay claim to be Wales's greatest Open Championship performer.

Thomas playing out a bunker during the 1968 Dunlop Masters at Royal Porthcawl

*(Media Wales)*

## Chapter Five
# Iestyn Tucker

WHETHER it be hacking the ball around an empty field or standing on the tee at St Andrews, every golfer dreams of hitting the 'perfect' shot. And during a career that has become legendary in Welsh amateur golf circles, Iestyn Tucker hit more than his fair share.

An astonishing 26 holes-in-one – one for each year of his Welsh international career – have been marked down on Tucker's cards throughout the piece, making for a fairly hefty bar bill at numerous clubhouses. He remembers where it all started:

'I got the first one at the age of nine at West Monmouthshire and it's certainly cost me a few drinks since then. I guess I've just been very lucky to find the bottom of the cup that often from the tee. I've never gone into the research in detail, but I'm told that no one in Britain has ever claimed as many aces, and only one person worldwide, apparently an American gentleman, has done so.'

William Iestyn (Bill) Tucker has become synonymous with golfing excellence and true sportsmanship, and those players who compete every year at Newport and Whitchurch in the Order of Merit event that bears his name, are encouraged to follow the same principles. In terms of longevity there are few in the men's amateur game in Wales to hold a candle to Tucker, and only Vicki Thomas in the women's game can lay claim to a longer international career.

That career was inspired by his father, who was both professional and greenkeeper at the West Monmouthshire golf club in Brynmawr. Perhaps it was the rarefied atmosphere of Britain's highest golf course – the 14th tee of the Ben Sayers designed layout stands more than 1,500 feet above sea level – that enabled Tucker to show promise even at the age of four when he was first given a cut-down club.

Born in 1927, Tucker was something of a child prodigy, that first hole-in-one at West Monmouthsire coming shortly before his father moved to a new post at the Palleg club, near Brecon. By the age of 11 he was knocking it around Palleg's nine holes in 36 shots and then continued his development back at West Monmouthshire when his father returned at the outbreak of World War Two. As the professional's son, the young Tucker was given courtesy of the course, and that allowed him the time to polish what was to become a simple and elegant golf swing which would serve him so well.

He joined the Royal Air Force Voluntary Reserve at the age of seventeen and spent four years in the service before returning home, and it was only at the age of 21 that he first started to play in club competitions. He was given his first handicap of six by the club committee but that was halved in just a week as he won his first competition.

And, remarkably, a week later he was off scratch after breaking the course record with a round of 69. Has there ever been a quicker route from non handicap to scratch golfer?

And reaching that magical scratch handicap was just the start, as Tucker would maintain or better it for the next forty years.

He continued his education at Loughborough College – he would go on to become a teacher – and appeared for the Leicestershire county team. He also set a new course record at Longcliffe, the second of seventeen course records he would hold throughout his career, the other sixteen at clubs in Wales.

He won the West Monmouthshire club championship at the very first attempt and, in 1948, he started to make an impact on the wider stage when he reached the quarter-finals of the Welsh Amateur Championship at Royal Porthcawl before losing to three-time champion Sam Roberts, of Prestatyn. He also tied for the Monmouthshire County title, which he would win outright in 1949.

By now he had joined the Monmouthshire club at Abergavenny, the start of an association that has lasted till today.

Keen observers were already becoming aware of his talent, but there was no indication of the outstanding career that would lie ahead of him when Tucker first appeared for Wales in 1949. Originally selected as a reserve, he was drafted into the team to face Scotland in the final match of the Home Internationals and contributed one-and-a-half points including a singles victory.

No one could have predicted that he would retain his place in the team every year until 1973 when a loss of form persuaded the selectors to drop him. He responded by winning back his place for the next two years before announcing his retirement:

'It's a record that I'm naturally very proud of, but whenever I played for Wales it was about the team and not about me as an individual. If you take in the four European Team Championships I played in, and a few other representative matches against Australia and France, I think my total appearances in foursomes and singles is 198.'

That is another of Tucker's records which is unlikely to be troubled in an era where the vast majority of amateur internationals decide to try their luck in the professional ranks.

As someone who openly admits that he never gave a second thought to turning pro, Tucker believes that some of today's generation would be better served by remaining in the amateur game for at least a while longer:

'A lot of the young lads today are turning professional at the first opportunity and, to be brutally honest, many of them don't have a hope of making it. It was something I never considered at any time. I remember in the 1960s I played an exhibition match at Cardiff golf club with another amateur Huw Squirrell and the professionals Dai Rees and Dave Thomas. I was fortunate to have a red-hot day and I set a new course record with a 65. Dai shot a 68, Dave a 69 and Huw a 74. Afterwards Dai asked me why I wasn't a professional and told me I could live with the players at that level any time. It was a great compliment but I was always happy with the way things were.'

Tucker, left, with Welsh team-mates John Llewellyn Morgan and Jeff Toye at Royal Porthcawl in 1962    *(Media Wales)*

Tucker was renowned as a great match player, although he admits that he actually preferred strokeplay competitions. Internationals aside, his matchplay record was most impressive as he won the Welsh Amateur Championship twice and competed in seven finals, a tally bettered only by Henry Howell from the Glamorganshire club, Penarth, who appeared in eight finals and won every one between 1920 and 1932.

Tucker's first triumph came at Southerndown in 1963 when he overcame John Povall in the final and he lifted the trophy again at Aberdovey in 1966, seeing off Ted Davies in the decider:

'I didn't have the greatest of records in finals and two out of seven isn't that impressive. But I was up against quality golfers and I always gave it my best shot. I would have liked to have won a few more but that's the nature of the game. I remember John Llewellyn Morgan was in irrepressible form in the 1951 final at Royal St David's and Alf Lockley's short game in the 1956 final at Southerndown was unbelievable.

'I always accepted defeat as graciously as possible and if the other man plays that well it is difficult to have any complaints.'

Naturally a modest man, Tucker has always played down his continual omissions from the Great Britain and Ireland Walker Cup teams, but many experts believe him to be one of the best players, if not the best, never to have appeared in the matches.

'There is some regret that I didn't make the Walker Cup team, of course,' he admits. 'I was twice in the squad and in 1953 I thought I was deserving of a place when I beat three of the team members in the Home Internationals.'

The selection process was undoubtedly far more 'political' in those days. Some said he was a victim of the selection politics and others claim that he didn't play in enough of the big events outside Wales to catch the attention of the selectors, his golf always being combined, and at times inevitably constrained, by his commitments as a physical education teacher.

But the simple principles of fairness and picking the best players for the job were implemented by Tucker himself years later when he was sitting on the Walker Cup selection panel:

'I suppose being a selector is the next best thing to actually playing in the matches and at least I can claim to have picked Colin Montgomerie for the side. He didn't go on to have a bad career, did he?'

His love of strokeplay saw him win sixteen Monmouthshire titles and his record in the Duncan Putter at Southerndown is peerless. In the eleven years following the inauguration of the tournament in 1959, Tucker was a winner four times and a runner-up four times. There were two more runner-up finishes secured in subsequent years. And the Welsh strokeplay title, which he had tried and failed to win for so many years, finishing second on three occasions, was finally captured in 1976 at Newport when Tucker was into his 50th year.

When Tucker finally hung up his clubs as an international in 1976, his involvement with Welsh golf was in no way ended as he embarked on an equally impressive career as an administrator, and made a major impact in Seniors' golf. When he called time on his playing career at the top level, Tucker was already sitting on the Welsh Golfing Union's council as a County representative. He went on to serve with distinction as Welsh captain, chairman of selectors, Walker Cup selector, vice-chairman, chairman and president.

The old competitive instinct served Tucker well as he won the Welsh Seniors' Championship in 1982, 1984 and 1989, the last of those coming after he had undergone major eye surgery:

'I enjoyed the Seniors' events as they were a great opportunity to catch up with so many old friends from the past. I'm not surprised in the least that Seniors' golf has become so popular the world over.'

The esteem and affection that Tucker is held in is borne out by the fact that he holds honorary life membership at four clubs and honorary membership at twelve more throughout Wales. He remains president of The Monmouthshire and, even into his 80s, he still travelled from his home in Merthyr Tydfil to play a few holes whenever possible.

In recent years his attendance at many of the major events has been restricted, but he remains in touch with the scene and his passion for Welsh golf is still as strong as ever.

'Golf has been very good to me and I have a lifetime of happy memories to look back on. There have been a few disappointments along the way but I suppose that is to be expected in any walk of life. I'd like to think I have given something back to the game in Wales because I was able to get so much out of it.

'Things have changed out of all recognition, especially with regard to the international players. These days most of them just see the amateur game as a stepping stone to professional golf. I suppose the only modern-day equivalent to me would be Nigel Edwards. Nigel has a job in golf which he is happy with and can still achieve all he wants to in the amateur game.

'I think the Welsh Golf Union and the new Golf Union of Wales have done a good job in moving along with the changing times and I'm sure they will continue to do so.'

In such changing times we are unlikely to see another Iestyn Tucker, the grand old man of Welsh golf.

# Chapter Six

# Brian Huggett

THERE will be no prouder Welshman than Brian Huggett when the first ball of the 2010 Ryder Cup is struck at the Celtic Manor Resort in Newport.

Brian George Charles Huggett, simply 'Mr Welsh Golf' to many, is not just passionate about his country and his sport, but can claim to have played a significant role in transforming the Ryder Cup from a mismatch that was dying on its feet to the world's third biggest sporting spectacle after the Olympic Games and the football World Cup.

Having played in six Ryder Cup teams himself without being on the winning side, Huggett captained the Great Britain and Ireland team beaten 12½-7½ by the Americans at Royal Lytham & St Annes in 1977. By then the GB&I team had won just three times in 22 attempts since the first official matches in 1927 and unless something was done the biennial contest – or no-contest – was in danger of falling into the sporting abyss.

As captain it was down to Huggett, along with another Ryder Cup veteran Peter Butler and the then European Tour president Lord Derby, to make representations to the USPGA with a view to changing the format:

'At first the Americans wanted the GB&I team to become a Rest of the World select, but we felt that such an amalgamation would be lacking in identity. We felt that a European side would have the identity we wanted and would be capable of giving the Americans a match. Also the European Tour was in its infancy and it was a great chance for us to boost its profile and its coffers. It just seemed like the natural progression. We had to put a good case forward or the event would have died a death.

'To be fair the Americans took on board what we were saying and recognised that players like Seve Ballesteros and Bernhard Langer were emerging and would be a big draw. The fact the event is now as big over there as it is in Europe shows we were right. It was the major turning point in the history of the Ryder Cup.'

Huggett, born in Porthcawl in 1936, played his formative golf at Neath, where he moved at the age of ten when his father, G.W. Huggett, who had been attached to Royal Porthcawl, became club professional. When he was 14 the family moved to Surrey, and just two years later Huggett became a professional himself, taking up an assistant's post with his father at Redhill and Reigate before moving to Sudbrook Park, Richmond. After completing his National Service, Huggett resumed his apprenticeship at West Sussex before spending two years at the Royal Hong Kong club.

Huggett pictured on the Ryder Cup Twenty10 course at Celtic Manor

*(Media Wales)*

His first significant tournament wins as a pro came in 1962 when he captured the Dutch Open title and the Singapore International. The Cox Moore title and the German Open followed in 1963, the same year he began his long association with the Ryder Cup.

The 26-year-old Welshman was selected for his GB&I debut against the Americans at East Lake, Atlanta, and, despite the 23-9 drubbing handed out to the visitors, Huggett had the sort of debut few will ever forget:

'Myself and George Will, both newcomers, were sent out in the opening foursomes against Arnold Palmer, who was at his peak, and rookie Johnny Pott. Most people thought we were the sacrificial lambs but the truth was they had a lot more pressure on them and a lot more to lose.

'Palmer was the best golfer in the world, but in foursomes you are only as good as your partner and we beat them 3&2.'

Huggett and fellow Welshman Dave Thomas gained a half in the second series of fourballs before he defeated Pott 3&1 in the singles to cap an excellent individual series.

From that moment on Huggett and the Ryder Cup seemed to go hand in glove as he would feature in five of the next six matches before taking over the captaincy.

In 1967 at the Champions Club in Houston, Texas, GB&I were again routed, this time 23½-8½, but Huggett was not disgraced as he contributed a rare singles point when defeating Julius Boros at the last. But perhaps the highlight came in 1969 at Royal Birkdale where Huggett was a central figure in a dramatic 16-16 tie.

In what became known as one of the most ill-tempered clashes in the history of the sport, trouble flared on the second afternoon when Huggett and the young Bernard Gallacher took on Dave Hill and Ken Still in the fourballs:

'There was trouble from the start. At the first I had a ten-foot putt for a three and Still chose to stand only six feet away from me wearing white shoes which clearly caught the eye. He wouldn't move away until I had to tell him to stand behind me. At the 7th, the Americans putted out of turn and when I told them, all hell broke loose. Still was arguing when we got to the 8th tee and although we didn't come to blows it was as near as you can get.'

The crowds turned against the Americans and Dai Rees, one of the stalwarts of the European game, had to try and quieten the spectators down with the help of the local constabulary.

Hill and Still took the match 2&1 but the controversy lingered on, although Huggett and Hill made their peace a week later when they both travelled to Seattle on the same flight to play in the Alcan tournament. The following day in the final round of singles matches Huggett faced Billy Casper and was faced with a five-foot 'knee trembler' on the 18th to halve the match.

Huggett holed it and famously burst into tears, believing his half was good enough to secure overall victory for GB&I. However, in the one remaining match on the course Tony Jacklin couldn't get the better of Jack Nicklaus and the American's sporting concession for a half ensured the overall result was square:

'To have beaten that American side which boasted Nicklaus, Casper, Lee Trevino and Ray Floyd to name but four would have been the most fantastic achievement. Having raced my first putt past the hole I knew just how crucial it was as I stood over the return. It wasn't the most difficult putt I ever had but certainly one of the most nervy. The emotion afterwards told its own story.'

In 1971 at the Old Warson Country Club in Missouri, Huggett and Jacklin enjoyed a memorable opening day, first defeating Nicklaus and Dave Stockton before halving with Trevino and Mason Rudolph in the afternoon. The final outcome was 18½-13½ to the USA.

By now one of the seasoned campaigners of the team, Huggett went through the 1973 series at Muirfield undefeated, although the matches finished with an all-too-predictable 19-13 American win. GB&I had actually led 5½-2½ after the opening day, the highlight of which was undoubtedly the 3&1 success for Huggett and Maurice Bembridge against the 'dream team' of Nicklaus and Palmer. The same pairing collected a win and a half on the second day before Huggett completed a superb individual series by seeing off Homero Blancas 4&2 at the top of the singles order.

On his final playing appearance, at Laurel Valley, Pennsylvania, in 1975, Huggett featured just once in the foursomes and fourballs, partnering Jacklin to a 3&2 win against Trevino and Bob Murphy. But there would be no fairy-tale ending as he went down 4&2 to Gene Littler in his final singles outing, and the Americans romped home once more 21-11.

There was, of course, far more to Huggett's career than the Ryder Cup. He won 16 times in Europe and chalked up more than 30 victories worldwide by the time he 'retired' from the Tour in 1980 to concentrate on his golf-course design business.

In 1967 he claimed the PGA Closed Championship and completed the double in 1968 when he added the News of the World PGA Matchplay. That was one of three victories in Europe that year, which saw Huggett finish as the leading money winner. His last two victories, the Portuguese Open in 1974 and the BA/Avis Open in 1978, came after the formal start of the European Tour – of which he was an ardent supporter – in 1972.

Huggett also had a couple of near misses at The Open Championship, finishing third behind Palmer at Royal Troon in 1962 and joint runner-up to Peter Thomson at Royal Birkdale in 1965.

'I don't lose any sleep over it,' says Huggett, 'because I didn't blow a chance of winning at either. I came second after finishing with a late flourish when I birdied four of the last six holes. I was already back in the clubhouse to watch Peter birdie the last two holes to finish two ahead of me. In those days you played 36 holes on the final day and it was the third round that cost me as I had three double-bogeys on my card.'

Huggett was awarded the MBE for services to his sport in 1978, the same year in which he fulfilled another ambition by winning the Welsh PGA Championship at Whitchurch, Cardiff. At 41 years of age Huggett prevailed in a sudden death play-off after finishing the 36-hole event tied with a promising youngster from Oswestry by the name of Ian Woosnam:

'It was a great moment because I'd been on the circuit for over 20 years and played for Wales in the World Cup but I'd always wanted to call myself a Welsh champion.'

In the dozen years following his decision to stop playing tournament golf, Huggett forged a reputation as one of the sport's leading course designers, creating layouts in some unlikely outposts including Iran. But the competitive juices began to flow again when the European Seniors' Tour was introduced in 1992.

Between 1992 and 2000 the 'Welsh Bulldog' as he became known, won ten titles including his own 'Major' at the 1998 Senior British Open at Royal Portrush. That triumph came at the age of 61 with Huggett giving ten years away to many of his rivals. He relishes the Seniors' Tour:

'It's been fantastic for me and for many other players. The camaraderie was great and it was a chance to meet up with so many old friends and renew a few old rivalries to boot. The putting wasn't as good as it had been a few years earlier but I played some decent golf and enjoyed every minute of it.'

In 2006 Huggett became only the fourth golfer to be inducted into the Welsh Sports Hall of Fame following Dai Rees, Dave Thomas and Vicki Thomas. His induction was all the more special as the same batch included his long-time friend Don Shepherd, the Glamorgan cricketing great. Huggett's love of cricket extends to a membership of the MCC.

Now into his seventies, but as sprightly and as sharp as ever, Huggett lives in Ross-on-Wye and is enjoying his latest role as an ambassador to Ryder Cup Wales 2010, as well as that of President at the magnificent Machynys Peninsula club near Llanelli. He has become one of the most recognisable faces of the Ryder Cup board, travelling far and wide to promote an event which he played such a key role in creating some 30 years earlier.

He has acted as an advisor on the construction of the Twenty Ten course, which is to host the matches, and retains an enthusiasm and drive which is totally infectious:

'I am absolutely committed to helping Wales get everything right for 2010. I think people are now beginning to realise just what it means for our little country to be hosting the world's third biggest sporting event.

'It is going to provide a massive boost to golf development, tourism and the whole economy. It is a once-in-a-lifetime opportunity to establish Wales as a premier golfing nation and we need to grasp it with both hands.'

It is fitting that the man who helped re-invent the Ryder Cup is now paving the way for what should be Welsh golf's finest hour.

Huggett driving off the first tee
at Royal Porthcawl
*(Media Wales)*

John Jermine

# Chapter Seven

# John Jermine

WHEN the post of Ryder Cup Wales chairman was advertised in 2002, there was no shortage of applicants from the very highest echelons of the sporting and business communities.

But few of the 100 or so contenders for the prestigious post could ever match the passion and commitment of the successful applicant, John Jermine. Bringing the third biggest sporting event on the sporting planet to such a small nation requires special qualities. And in Jermine those qualities are crystal clear for all to see.

Born in the Cardiff suburb of Radyr in 1944, Jermine has been involved in Welsh golf at virtually every level, although it was tennis that first attracted him to the sporting arena.

'I used to play tennis with two friends, Pete Grundy and Nigel Morgan, and both their sets of parents were members at Radyr Golf Club,' he recalled. 'I joined Radyr at the age of ten and eventually played more and more golf. I gave up tennis in 1960 when I left school and concentrated solely on golf.'

It was at Radyr that Jermine forged the first of many firm friendships – and rivalries – in the sport with another of the most familiar names on the Welsh scene, Jeff Toye. The pair played team golf together but also went head-to-head in the club championship on numerous occasions, as Jermine remembers well:.

'We won the club title four times each but then Toye had to go back about ten years later and nick another one!'

Having trained as a chartered accountant and taken his first steps into the business world, Jermine moved to South Africa in 1969, returning to Britain eighteen months later and making his first impression on the Welsh international selectors.

His first international appearance was in 1972 at Royal Troon but, as Jermine explained, it was far different to the relative luxury that today's leading players enjoy:

'It's a measure of how far golf has come that in those days, when you were chosen for Wales, you were given a badge but had to find a blazer on which to have it sewn. I had to go out and find a tailor and have a blazer made to match the free badge.'

Jermine was to become a fixture in the Welsh team from 1972 to 1977, playing in two European Championships in Killarney and The Hague, before increasing business commitments and a young family changed his priorities from the golf course to the home and office environments.

'I didn't play much at all between 1982 and 1990, and then Andy Morgan, the

John Jermine pictured following his appointment
as Chairman of Ryder Cup Wales 2010

*(Media Wales)*

President of the Welsh Golfing Union at the time, asked me if I'd be prepared to captain the Welsh Boys' team.'

The following year Jermine's young charges tied for the Home Internationals title at Royal Mid Surrey, the first time Wales had won a team event at any level. And twelve months later, in the unlikely surroundings of the Marianske Lazne resort in the Czech Republic, an even more significant step was taken.

Now in charge of the senior international side, Jermine captained Wales to the European Team Championship crown.

'They were a wonderful team and it remains one of the best moments of my life in golf and one of the best things that ever happened to me,' said Jermine.

While Jermine was steering a group of talented young players to European glory, he, along with Morgan and his colleagues at the Welsh Golfing Union, were also laying down the foundations for future success by implementing programmes that were revolutionary in Wales at the time:

'I brought in Luther Blacklock from Woburn and he, alongside national coach Craig Defoy, taught a lot of the Welsh players who are now making an impact in the professional game. Will James was an exceptional sports psychologist, John Garland looked after the players' short games and we also had fitness and nutritional back-up.'

Having reached levels that were way above anything achieved in Wales before, Jermine reluctantly stepped down as captain in 1996 as business commitments again came calling.

Ironically, relinquishing the role to Tony Disley ultimately allowed Jermine to play more golf himself, which led to one remarkable week in the summer of 2000 when, at the age of 56, he won the Welsh Amateur Championship at Royal St David's, Harlech.

'I was extremely lucky to win there and I surprised the whole of Wales, not least myself. I will always be exceptionally proud of the fact that at 56 I was the oldest player to have won a national championship, not just in Britain, but in the world.

'The Castle Cottage in Harlech, owned by Glyn and Jacquie Roberts, is perhaps my favourite hotel anywhere but I had only booked to stay for one night as I was due to play the young Welsh international David Price in the first round. I was fully expecting to drive home the next day but I just kept on winning.

'My favourite wine at the time was a Cloudy Bay Sauvignon Blanc 1998 and Glyn had four bottles in the hotel which I asked him to put to one side for me. I told him I'd have one bottle a night and take the rest home with me as I wouldn't be staying long. I ended up having them all and for a 56-year-old schoolboy it was the week of my life.

'The weather was awful when I played Pricey, it was pouring with rain. He was a much better player than I was, but I chipped and putted hole after hole to stay only one behind him. Then, and I'll never forget it, when I holed yet another putt at the 12th he put his umbrella down, walked to the next tee getting soaked and I thought, "Gotcha."

'My best win of the week, though, was against Craig Williams, perhaps the outstanding player in Wales at the time. Craig went round St David's in 65 and I still beat him, although no one to this day, including me, quite knows just how I managed it.

'On the Saturday morning the weather was lovely for the final against Richard Brookman, and I was one down at lunch with Brooky playing some good golf. But then the wind picked up and I managed to beat him too. I always seem to play my best in the worst weather and that week everything went for me.

'Most of the youngsters didn't realise I could actually play. Many of them had been in the teams I had captained and they probably thought I was just the old fella who booked the hotel rooms and arranged the meals.

'But they were all wonderful to me and it's a week I shall never, ever forget.'

Jermine played in the Home Internationals at Carnoustie later in the year, but with his furniture retailing business being hit hard by the fuel strike, concentrating on the golf was far from easy. That was to be Jermine's final appearance in senior Welsh colours, but his impact on the game in Wales was far from over.

'The Ryder Cup Wales Chairman's post was advertised in 2002 and a friend suggested I might like to apply. He thought it was the type of job I'd do quite well and would want to do. So I applied, was lucky enough to be appointed and I have enjoyed every minute of it.

'It represents the best ever chance to push the sport forward and make Wales a genuine golfing destination to rival some of the finest in the world. Working with the Celtic Manor Resort, Visit Wales and the Welsh Assembly Government has been a marvellous experience. We are the smallest nation ever to host the Ryder Cup and 2010 will hopefully be one of this country's greatest success stories.'

While he has lived outside Wales since 1974 – he is now based at Sunningdale in Berkshire – Jermine's passion for his homeland remains undiminished, and you sense that he is never happier than when he is striding the fairways of one of the four Welsh courses that have played such a major part in his life.

'I'm a life member as Radyr and honoured at have been awarded such status. Radyr was designed by Harry Colt, who also designed the Sunningdale New course and Pine Valley, which is rated as one of the very best in the USA. So whenever I play there I'm aware of it being this little hidden gem that we have in Wales.

'Southerndown I joined for winter golf in 1962. I won the club championship there in 1965 and have had a love affair with the golf club ever since, winning the Duncan Putter twice, in 1975 and 1983 and coming second in 1969, tied with a certain Peter Oosterhuis.

'As for Royal Porthcawl, which has become known to my daughters as 'daddy's little square of heaven,' it is my favourite place in the world and the most beautiful golf course I've ever come across. You can view the sea from every tee and every green, and I've been a member there since 1976 and still make time to spend six or seven weekends there each year. As I drive down towards the entrance gates, with the sea on my left, I know that for the next four or five hours it will be pure pleasure, no matter how well or badly I play.

'Royal St David's, Harlech, is my second favourite place, and if I had been born in the north it probably would have been roles reversed with Porthcawl.'

As a member of the Welsh Golfing Union council, Jermine played a key administrative role in the game for many years and, as President-elect of the Union he oversaw the merger of the WGU and the Welsh Ladies' Golfing Union into the new Golf Union of Wales, formed in January 2007.

But for all his skills as a businessman and a sports administrator, Jermine has never lost sight of the fact that golf is a game to be played and to be enjoyed, and seeing Welsh players hit the heights in both the amateur and professional ranks sparks a relentless wave of enthusiasm in him.

'During my time as captain of the Welsh boys and senior teams, I had a total of 47 players in my charge, and as well as a spate of amateur successes, seven of them have gone on to gain full European Tour cards. And I can honestly say that every single one of them was a pleasure to work with.

'There was a time when Welsh expectations were just too low, but the work that was done with the players who are now doing so well on the world stage has paid handsome dividends. Now we are seeing young Welsh players who are comfortable playing on the toughest golf courses and against the toughest competition.'

Despite his extensive commitments off the course, Jermine has no intention of hanging up his golf bag and exchanging his spikes for a comfy pair of slippers.

'After I won the Welsh title I played very little golf. I really didn't know what to do next. I couldn't get my head around playing Seniors' golf because that starts at 55 and at 56 I still wanted to be playing 'proper' golf. Then I hurt my arm in the gym and it took about a year for me to recover to the extent where I could swing a club comfortably again. By that time the magic had dwindled a bit but then I worked at it again and in the next year or so I was playing better than I have for a long time.

'I finally came to my senses at the age of 63 and decided to start playing old age pensioners' golf and had a go at a few of the Seniors' events. And I'm hopeful that I can play some decent golf for a few more years yet.'

Decent golf is probably a touch modest as Jermine was good enough to win both the Welsh and English Seniors' Championships in 2008, becoming the first Welshman to capture the English title. That after he had been runner-up in the Welsh Seniors' in 2007.

On the course and off it, the chairman of the board remains a key figure in the development of the game in Wales.

John Jermine (centre), with the victorious 1993 Welsh Team from the European Championships in the Czech Republic. L-R Richard Dinsdale, Bradley Dredge, Calvin O'Carroll, Craig Evans and Mike Macara (Richard Johnson absent from photograph)

*(Media Wales)*

# Chapter Eight
# Craig Defoy

BORN in the USA, but definitely made in Wales, Craig Defoy can take much of the credit for developing what is widely recognised to be the Principality's most talented, and successful, crop of players to date.

Naturally modest, Defoy would be quick to spread the bouquets around, but during his ten-year tenure as the Welsh Golfing Union's National Coach, he implemented a structure that shaped the careers of the likes of Phil Price, Stephen Dodd and Bradley Dredge. His foresight, planning and persuasive skills dragged the development of the sport in Wales up by its bootstraps and, although they may not even realise it, today's generation of 'professional' amateurs owe Defoy a debt of thanks.

Born in the Eastern seaboard state of Pennsylvania in 1947 of an American father and Welsh mother, Defoy crossed the Atlantic at the age of just six months as the family set up home in Burry Port, the picturesque village just outside Llanelli. The famous Ashburnham links were right on his doorstep although Defoy, who played out a host of sporting triumphs in the streets with his friends, admits that he had a less than conventional introduction to the game that would dominate his life.

'I heard there was a golf competition going on (which turned out to be the PGA Championship) and also heard that if you went along and pulled a trolley round you'd get a few bob for it. I couldn't get down there quick enough and I asked the first player I saw if I could caddy for him. I was hooked almost instantly.'

When a new professional, Richard Playle, arrived at Ashburnham and began to take more of an interest in the junior section, Defoy's own game steadily improved and the seeds of his ambition to make a career from the sport were sown.

The family moved to Middlesex when Defoy was fifteen but the ambitions remained the same. His schooling ended on a Friday afternoon in 1963 – the year after he made his only appearance in the Welsh Boys' championship at Harlech – when he completed his O-Level examinations. Remarkably, his professional career started the following Monday when he signed up as an assistant to Bill Cox at Fulwell Golf Club.

'I spent seven or eight hours a day picking up balls and making the tea but it was a stepping stone and I was determined to make the most of it.'

His apprenticeship underway, Defoy's next move would be one that took his career to a completely new level.

'I got a call telling me about Dick Burton (the 1939 Open Championship winner) who was head pro at Coombe Hill. He took a great interest in anyone with

Defoy waiting to tee off in the 1997 Welsh professional championship

*(Media Wales)*

the ambition to be a tournament player, and had a stable that already included Neil Coles, Tony Grubb and Hugh Boyle. Dick gave me a job there and then and immediately I was surrounded by better players, received plenty of encouragement, and started to develop quickly. He asked me how much money I had to my name, which was about £100, and then he told me to go off, play tournaments, and only come back when the money ran out.'

Defoy was to spend 10 years under Burton at Coombe Hill, a period that straddled the introduction of the European Tour in 1971.

Burton was one of three Open champions from Coombe Hill, Sandy Herd and the great Henry Cotton the others, and Defoy had his moment in the sun in 1971 at Royal Birkdale, finishing in fourth place, three shots behind 'Super Mex' Lee Trevino.

'People always ask me about it but I was never really going to win it. Trevino was in control but to be up there on the leaderboard on the final day is something I will always remember.

'In those days Tony Jacklin and Peter Oosterhuis were the only two British players who were really expected to be challenging at the Majors so it was a great thrill. I absolutely loved the experience and maybe I should have gone on from there but in truth my game never developed as much as I expected it to. I was someone who people started looking out for after The Open but it didn't really happen for me. That's the nature of sport. Sometimes you don't reach the heights you aspire to.'

After leaving Coombe Hill, Defoy spent seven years at Bryn Meadows, then a spell at Calcot Park, before moving back to Coombe Hill in 1981.

During his tournament career he won four Welsh PGA titles in 1975, 1977, 1981 and 1982, claimed five victories on the African Tour and represented his county in seven World Cups. He also played twice for the Great Britain and Ireland club professionals in the PGA Cup. So, while his European Tour career may not have lived up to its early promise, Defoy was no stranger to the winners enclosure.

With that sort of experience it was no surprise that Defoy was sounded out by the Welsh Golfing Union in 1986 when they were looking to appoint their first national coach.

'I think Brian Huggett and myself were in the frame and to be honest I had thought Brian would be favourite for it. But the Union got in touch and asked me if I would be interested in doing the job. At the time, the major concern was that Wales had a lot of talent but, for want of a better word, the whole system needed to be more professional.

'When I started out I was a little shocked, and a little disappointed at how far behind Wales was in certain aspects of the game, things that looking back now it's quite hard to believe. For instance the players never paced the courses before events to get accurate yardages, something that the pros did without thinking, and something no player would be without now.

'We introduced fitness and nutritional programmes to the players, and I brought in Alan Fine, the leading sports psychologist at the time. Alan had a big impact on the players and Phil Price went on to use him to great effect in his professional career.

'The early years were frustrating at times because I felt that we weren't going in the right direction. I was seeing players who, despite having low handicaps, were actually lacking in the basics of golf. I felt that my remit was to polish these players and turn them into the finished article, not to be looking at things as fundamental as their grips and stances.'

Lesser men would have cut their losses but Defoy stuck at it and eventually the system that would revolutionise Welsh golf started to fall into place.

'We set up a dragnet policy to identify every Welsh qualified player at the age of twelve with a handicap of 24 or better. Those players were able to register on the Welsh Golfing Union coaching scheme and, for just £5, they were able to earn a diploma and get £20 worth of free tuition from their local pro. We worked with all the junior organisers around Wales to monitor players, the area coaches had their input and then, at the top of the pyramid, we had Luther Blacklock and John Garner working with the elite.

'It might not seem like it today, but of its time this was a very sophisticated set-up. And it was a model that has been adopted and adapted to some degree by a lot of other governing bodies.'

Defoy had to swim against some strong currents to get such a system in place, and he is thankful that the forward-thinking members of the Welsh Golfing Union at the time held sway over the traditionalists.

'I was fortunate that I had backing from a core of influential people who realised that we had to do something radical to buck the trend of mediocrity. I will always be grateful to them because I wouldn't have got anywhere with the policy otherwise. When I mentioned the term 'sports psychologist' there were some who turned their heads and wanted nothing to do with it, but once you start to see results, attitudes can change and even the most sceptical can be won over.

'It was a period of my life that I absolutely loved and my one regret is that my commitments at Coombe Hill didn't allow me to spend as much time as I would have liked on my work with the WGU.'

It was being appointed Director of Golf at Coombe Hill, where his wife Christina was also club secretary, which eventually forced Defoy, reluctantly, to end his association with the WGU. But as one door closed another opened, in the shape of the newly-created European Seniors' Tour.

Defoy with the trophy after winning the 1977 Welsh PGA title

*(Media Wales)*

'We were so busy at Coombe Hill that I hadn't really intended to play because I was spending much of my time sat behind a desk. You could say I peaked early as I finished runner-up in the first two events of the 1997 season and after that the club gave me their blessing to go and play on the tour full-time. It was too good an opportunity to miss.'

Defoy was to become a fixture on the Tour for the next ten years, his playing career interrupted only by an eighteen-month break in 1995 when he was diagnosed with a cancer, from which he thankfully recovered and went into remission. He went on to play more than 100 tournaments on the Seniors' Tour and after he retired from competition, maintained an interest through his seat on the Tour's board. He was edged out by Maurice Bembridge in the vote for the Chairmanship in 2007 but insists he will always view the Tour with great affection.

'If I'd been voted in as chairman I think I'd have still played in a few tournaments and attended as many others as possible, but I didn't begrudge Maurice the post. He was still playing regularly and has done a fine job for the Tour.'

Now living in Ferndown, having retired from his post at Coombe Hill in 2006, Defoy is enjoying a quiet life in one of the country's most beautiful areas. His skills as a coach are still in use, as he passes on his expertise to family and friends, and also helps out with the junior section at Ferndown.

Defoy has also been a keen supporter of the Ryder Cup Wales 2010 Legacy Fund, which has been put in place to safeguard the long-term development of the sport in the Principality. But he is just as happy digging the garden and taking the dog for a walk, as well as keeping an eye on the fortunes of his beloved Tottenham Hotspur.

Sons Simon, now based in Perth, Western Australia, and Warren, both followed their father into the world of professional golf. And one of Defoy's proudest moments remains the 1982 Welsh PGA Championship at Ashburnham when he and Simon played in the same tournament.

That pride also extends to seeing the names of his former charges at the top of leaderboards around the world.

'To see what Phil Price, Stephen Dodd and Bradley Dredge have done gives me a lot of satisfaction and hopefully there is a lot more to come from them. And if I played a small part in that, my involvement was more than worthwhile.'

Structures and development plans are now implemented at every level of the sport in Wales, but without Defoy's input who knows where things might have headed?

He was a forward thinker and Welsh golf will be forever grateful for his involvement.

# Chapter Nine

# Vicki Thomas

MANY golfers can claim to have re-written the record books at some stage in their careers. Vicki Thomas, on the other hand, has done so enough times to fill a whole library.

In fact, you could probably trawl the world and struggle to find a player with a record to match the undisputed queen of the Welsh women's game: eight Welsh Championship titles; six successive Curtis Cup appearances; the first player to appear in three winning Great Britain and Ireland Curtis Cup teams; an astonishing 28 consecutive years in the Welsh team. The list goes on and on.

And, even into her fifties, this bubbly and irrepressible character was still unearthing records that she didn't even realise she had set.

'I got a call from someone in 2007 telling me that there was a player in one of the English counties who had appeared in the County side during 36 seasons. Well, if my calculations were right, then I'd been in the Glamorgan side 37 times from my first appearance in 1970. I think the other lady might have been disappointed when she found out.'

That episode is a perfect snapshot of Thomas. The ultimate competitor, but someone who has always recognised that sport is, first and foremost, to be enjoyed.

'It's not life or death and like anything else, if you get too wrapped up in it all, you start to lose the enjoyment. I love playing golf and I've always accepted that I'm going to get a few bad days, although luckily I've had many more good ones.'

It was that same attitude which enabled Thomas to remain philosophical when she finally got the telephone call in 1999 which signalled the end of her remarkable run in the Welsh team.

'I was hoping to get to 30 successive appearances but when I received the telephone call from the Welsh Ladies' Golf Union, I took the view that it had to come at some stage. The Welsh girls had just won the junior Home Internationals for the first time so I can understand why they decided that was the time to pick a batch of youngsters ahead of a 44-year-old.'

So where did that incredible journey start? Born in Bargoed in 1954, the young Vicki Rawlings was always a keen participant in sport and was an exceptionally talented junior hockey player.

'My dad (Granville Rawlings) took up golf because his boss at work played, and he became a pretty good player himself. I started to mess about hitting a few shots. Myself and my sister Kerri then joined the Bargoed club, and dad started to teach us the basics of the game. When it got to a stage where he couldn't teach me any more, I started seeing the professional at Llanishen, Jack Taylor, and then I was coached by Sid Mouland at the Glamorganshire club, Penarth.'

The first title for the teenage Rawlings was the Welsh Girls' Championship in 1973 but, by her own admission, she was far from being the finished article.

'I remember playing in junior events and I was off a handicap of 18. The thing was, my father insisted that school work came first and golf second.'

It was in 1979 that she won the first of her Welsh titles at Conwy, and the Rawlings family created a little piece of Welsh sporting history. As well as winning the title, Vicki, Kerri, youngest sister Mandy and mother Joyce were all part of the Bargoed quintet who captured the Welsh Team crown. (For the record the odd woman out was Cheryl Norman.)

By that time she had graduated from university and was teaching physical education at Bedwas Comprehensive. The following year Vicki was beaten in the semi-finals of the Welsh Championship at Tenby by rising star Mandy, who would go on to win it and then retain it in 1981 at Royal St David's.

Now married to husband Graham Thomas and having moved to Swansea, Vicki won five of the next six Welsh titles playing out of Pennard, with whom she enjoyed a 21-year-association.

The remarkable dominance of the Rawlings family in the Welsh Championship between 1979 and 1987 was interrupted only in 1984 when the diminutive Sharon Roberts won at Newport. But those glory days of the early 1980s may not have materialised had it not been for Thomas's move and change of lifestyle.

'When I started living in Swansea, I found there were not too many teaching opportunities about at the time so I decided that I would take a year off work, play as much as I could and see how good I could get.

Thomas had already ascended to the ranks of GB&I, playing in the first of six Vagliano Trophies against the Continent of Europe in 1979, and the first of four Commonwealth Tournaments later in the same year. It was no surprise, therefore, when she was called up for a Curtis Cup debut in 1982, but it didn't exactly go as Thomas had planned, GB&I on the wrong end of a 14½-3½ hammering in Denver. Thomas played only once, in the final round of singles, where she was beaten 5&4 by Judy Oliver.

She may not have played anything like as big a part as she wanted to, but Thomas has always recognised that in team golf the sum is greater than its individual parts. And that is what has made her the ultimate team player.

'I love team golf and I think my personality and attitude has always been suited to it. Whether I win or lose my matches, the result still depends on how everyone else performs. I think I've been a pretty good team player over the years. There is something about matchplay that gets the adrenalin going, you never quite know what is going to happen next. To be honest if I had to play 72-holes of medal play week-in-week out, I would never have competed for this length of time.'

In 1984 Thomas did have a role among the cast leaders as GB&I redressed the balance somewhat of the humiliating defeat in Denver with a narrow 9½-8½ reverse at Muirfield. Thomas played in two of the four series and claimed 1½ points. Then, at Prairie Dunes, Kansas, in 1986, Thomas enjoyed what she considers to be the highlight of her Curtis Cup career as GB&I recorded an historic 13-5 victory.

'We became the first British team, men's or women's, to win on American soil and it was a fantastic achievement as the USA had what many thought to be one of their strongest ever teams.'

At Royal St George's, Sandwich, in 1988, GB&I retained the cup with an 11-7 win, Thomas, taking two-and-a-half points out of three to play a key role. But the USA restored what they believed was the status quo in 1990 at Somerset Hills, New Jersey. They prevailed 14-4 with Thomas playing out two epic singles with the great Carol Semple-Thompson, winning one and losing one.

Finally, at Royal Liverpool in 1992, Thomas made history when she was part of a third winning GB&I team in a 10-8 thriller. She didn't have the best of times individually, with one win from three matches, but the only result that really mattered to her was the overall one.

Thomas had won a record seventh Welsh title in 1991, eclipsing the mark set by the great Nancy Wright, who was at Royal St David's to see her achieve it, and had been part of the 1990 GB&I team at the Espirito Santo Trophy (The World Championships), a victory in the British Open Strokeplay at Strathaven clinching her place.

Thomas's decision to take a year off from full-time work actually lasted the best part of fifteen years. In the interim she worked as a supply teacher and did shifts behind the bar at Pennard Golf Club and with the Post Office among others, to fund her golf.

'I suppose you could call me a semi-professional and in many ways golf became a second career for me.'

Thomas was a regular visitor to the USA in the winter, where she became a successful performer on the Orange Blossom Tour. That kept her game sharp enough to ensure she was able to come out firing on all cylinders season after season.

The first indication that her glorious international career was on the down turn came in 1994 when, despite winning an eighth Welsh title and having already won the South Atlantic Championship in the States and another Glamorgan crown, the Curtis Cup selectors left her out of the team to travel to Tennessee. At the age of 39, she was still playing at an exceptionally high level and to many the decision came as a major shock.

Vicki Rawlings, right, with father Granville, mother Joyce and sisters Kerri and Mandy in 1979

(Media Wales)

'It was devastating at the time but these things happen in all sports. I felt I had done enough to make the team but the selectors thought otherwise.'

That news came in the same week Nancy Wright passed away at her home in Ffestiniog at the age of 77.

Thomas, rather than dwell on her own disappointment, put her clubs in the car and travelled north to Porthmadog to compete for Pennard in the Welsh Team Championship.

Her international career with Wales continued until 1998, by which time she had set benchmarks that will surely never be equalled.

Add to her CV eleven Glamorgan County titles in four different decades, three Welsh Open Strokeplay Championships, nine European Team Championship appearances for Wales, a New Zealand Open Strokeplay title and a New Zealand Foursomes title with Jill Thornhill, and you get some idea of her status not just in Welsh golf, but Welsh sport in general. Indeed, in 1998 she was inducted into the

Welsh Sports Hall of Fame in the same intake that included rugby legend Gareth Edwards and soccer great Cliff Jones.

During her glory years Thomas used to train once a week with Swansea City's professional footballers to ensure she kept in peak condition, but she never really gave full-time professional golf more than a cursory thought.

'It's something I often get asked about, especially now that you see so many of the youngsters turning pro at the first opportunity. For me the chance to travel the world at someone else's expense, to play team golf at the highest possible standard and to make friendships that last a lifetime has always been worth more to me than money. Maybe if the same opportunities that exist now had been available then, I might have thought differently.'

After the curtain finally came down on her international career, few would have begrudged Thomas the chance to sit back, relax and just enjoy a social round of golf with friends.

But Vicki Thomas is a competitor, and the next level of competition was Seniors' golf.

'I was fortunate Wales came into line with the other home nations and reduced the starting age for Seniors' golf from 55 to 50. It meant that I didn't have too long to wait.'

She won her first Welsh Women's Seniors' title in 2005 and by the time she had won it again in 2009 Thomas was halfway to matching her record Welsh title haul in Over-50s golf.

Thomas helped Wales to victory in the Seniors' Home International at Irvine in 2008 and became British Seniors' Open Strokeplay Champion at Pyle and Kenfig in 2009.

Throw in three Irish Open Seniors' titles for good measure and you can understand why the term 'competitive' could have been created just for Thomas.

'It's fantastic to meet up with so many of the old faces and I especially enjoy the Home Internationals because it's so relaxed yet the golf is still of a good competitive standard,' reflected Thomas.

Now based in Carmarthen and still working as a supply teacher, Thomas has no plans to walk away from competitive golf any time soon, and you wouldn't bet against her winning eight Welsh Seniors' titles just for the symmetry of it all.

'I would like to take on the role of captain to the Welsh women's team at some point because I think I would have a lot to offer the younger players. But I've always said that I can't do it while I'm still playing regularly.'

Given her almost unquenchable thirst for competition, that role on the sidelines may have to wait a while yet.

# Chapter Ten
# Tegwen Matthews

NOT many teenagers get the chance to travel the world and rub shoulders with Hollywood 'A' listers. But Tegwen Perkins – Wales's first Curtis Cup representative – did just that.

Perkins, now Tegwen Matthews, was hardly out of the spotlight during a glorious amateur career which saw her become one of the most recognisable faces in Welsh sport.

She was blazing a trail in 1975 when she was one of the top amateurs competing against the world's best women professionals in the Colgate Championships at Sunningdale. And when she turned up for the celebrity pro-am which preceded the event, there was quite a shock in store.

'I remember arriving at the course and Vicki Rawlings (now Thomas) asked me if I'd seen the start list. She told me I was playing with Bing Crosby, and at first I didn't believe it. Then I had a look myself and there it was. What a great thrill.'

The young Perkins couldn't have dreamed she would be moving in such exalted circles when she first started to hit a few golf balls at Wenvoe Castle. Born in Cardiff in 1955, she was, like so many successful players, introduced to the sport by her father Gwyn.

'He was a useful amateur footballer who then took up golf at Wenvoe. He was always one who believed that if you were going to do something you did it properly, so he became quite a decent player himself and was down to an eight handicap just a year after starting.

'I was about 12 when I first went along to the club with him and just started to hit a few balls around with some of the other girls for fun. The local pro thought that I showed some promise and in my very first Welsh Girls' Championship, at Wenvoe, I reached the semi-finals.'

At the start of 1969 Mr Perkins, keen to see his daughter fulfil the obvious potential that she was showing, got in touch with Leslie King, who ran a renowned golf school in London's Belgravia and was already working with the likes of Michael Bonallack, who went on to become one of Britain's great amateurs and secretary of the R&A, and Peter Townsend.

'I'll never forget the first time we saw Mr King. My father had taught me a lot of the basics of the game and he was quite proud of the way I swung the club. I stepped onto the mat and hit a few shots before Mr King announced that my swing was 'a load of rubbish. Given his reputation, we decided to take a leap of faith and go with him as he wanted to totally re-model my swing.'

Perkins in action for Great Britain and Ireland during the 1980 Curtis Cup matches at St Pierre

*(Media Wales)*

King, something of a golfing guru in the 1960s and 1970s, was not everyone's cup of tea but the Perkins' decision to run with him soon yielded some remarkable dividends. From a handicap of 30 Perkins came down to eight within two years and was down to two by 1972. And the summer after she started the weekly 300-mile round trips to London, Perkins won the Welsh Girls' Championship and started to feature in the junior international teams.

'Up to that point the senior Welsh team had featured a lot of older players, but the WLGU took a gamble and decided to put juniors like myself, Vicki Rawlings and Pam Light (now Chugg), into the side. To be playing against senior women at the ages of fourteen or fifteen was a fantastic learning experience and in selecting us, the Union took a gamble that paid off.'

Now emerging as one of the leading players in Wales, Perkins was also starting to make some moves on the wider GB&I stage. The Leslie King regime, taking a broader approach to golf which was considered radical at the time, also included a conditioning programme and it was not unusual for Perkins to be up earlier than most of her contemporaries, working on stretching and strengthening exercises.

The proof of the pudding was in the results she started to achieve, 1973 seeing Perkins win the South Western Championship, the Worplesdon Foursomes with Richard Evans and the prestigious Wills International Matchplay title at Wentworth. There was also a runners-up spot in the Welsh Girls' Championship and a joint fourth in the British Strokeplay.

The GB&I selectors could hardly ignore such a record and Perkins was selected to make her debut in the Vagliano Trophy against the Continent of Europe in Eindhoven, Holland.

Back home she polled enough votes to finish second in the Welsh Sports Personality of the Year awards, Commonwealth Games gold-medal winning athlete Berwyn Price edging her out. She was to become a regular in the top ten at the awards during the mid-1970s, and that in itself was an achievement given some of the competition.

'The following year I was third and Gareth Edwards won it, so it was amazing to be mentioned in the same breath as someone who was a rugby legend worldwide. Golf didn't enjoy the profile then that it does now so they were really special occasions.'

When she was selected to tour South Africa as part of a four-strong GB&I team in March of 1974, a Curtis Cup appearance later in the year looked a formality. But the eighteen-year-old was named only as a non-travelling reserve for the eight player team, and while the rest headed to San Francisco, Perkins headed to the West Country to represent Glamorgan in the County Finals at Burnham and Berrow.

'There was disappointment but then, after playing on the second morning, I got the news that Ann Irwin had a back injury and I was being called up as cover. By lunchtime I was on my way to the States.

'I didn't play on the opening morning but Jenny Lee Smith was unwell so I made my debut in the singles and managed a half with a very good opponent, Cindy Hill.'

In doing so she became the first Welsh woman to appear in the event.
Perkins took a point in the foursomes the following day and although she lost her singles, and GB&I lost the match 13-5, it had been an eventful and more than satisfactory debut at this level.

A whirlwind year was far from over, Perkins spending another month in the USA before returning home to reach the final of the British Girls' Championship where she was beaten by Ruth Barry and finishing runner-up in the British Ladies' Strokeplay. Then it was off to the Dominican Republic for the Espirito Santo Trophy, where she was part of a silver medal-winning GB&I team.

By 1975 Perkins had finished her schooling and was working in the family shop in Cardiff and the inevitable questions about turning professional began to emerge.

'I was keen to have the opportunity to play as much golf as I could, but at the time there was no established women's European Tour so turning professional meant going to America full-time.

'I was approached on one occasion by the management company IMG, but I decided that staying an amateur was the best for me. If I had to make the decision 30 years on, with the game as it is today, I'm sure it would have been different and I'd have given it a serious go.'

Perkins retained her place in the Vagliano Trophy team for 1975, and later that year the Curtis Cup team was selected for the matches at Royal Lytham & St Annes in 1976, and the Welsh girl didn't have to rely on a late call-up this time.

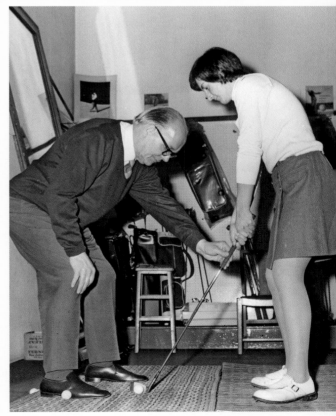

A young Tegwen Perkins with teaching guru Leslie King at his Belgravia clinic in 1973                    *(Media Wales)*

If she needed any extra motivation to prove her worth, it was provided by the well-known professional Vivien Saunders.

'After the team was selected she wrote an article in one of the broadsheets saying that everyone merited their selection apart from Tegwen Perkins. I found that pretty strange and as it turned out, I was the leading points scorer in the 1976 Curtis Cup so I guess she got it wrong.'

She actually won three points out of four, losing only at the last hole to Debbie Massey in an 11½-6½ overall defeat.

Perkins claimed her first Welsh Women's title during the memorable summer of 1976, defeating Ann Johnson in the final at Royal Porthcawl. From there she went on to win a maximum six points out of six in the Home Internationals, the first time such a feat had been achieved. For her efforts Perkins, along with Jenny Lee Smith, was joint recipient of the DAKS Woman Golfer of the Year award.

At the start of the 1977 season, Perkins and her great friend Mary McKenna, a legendary figure in Irish golf, headed off to America once again to play on the highly competitive Orange Blossom Tour. That was a precursor to a campaign which saw her retain the Welsh title, defeating Pamela Whitley in the final at Aberdovey, capture the Avia Foursomes with McKenna and secure a third successive Vagliano Trophy team place.

There was to be a third successive Curtis Cup in 1978 as part of the GB&I team beaten 12-6 by the USA in New York, and a fourth straight Vagliano Trophy in 1979 by which time she had married and become Tegwen Thomas.

'By 1979 I felt I wasn't playing as well as I had been a few years earlier and work commitments were becoming greater.'

It was a testament to her determination and natural ability that she remained at the top level of the sport for several more years, with a fourth Curtis Cup appearance in 1980 at St Pierre, Chepstow. Unfortunately there was to be no 'home' win as the USA prevailed once again, this time by a 13-5 margin.

A Welsh international career that had started back in 1971 eventually ended with her final appearance in the Home Internationals in 1983. By then there were also two appearances for GB&I in the Commonwealth Tournament, three South Western titles and eight Glamorgan Championship wins on the CV.

'I admire those players who carry on for as long as they can, but for me the time was right to leave and I wanted to go out while I was still at a high level.'

Still only in her late twenties when she 'retired', Thomas pursued her career in the financial sector, spending seventeen years with Lloyds and seven with First Plus before linking up with Picture Finance.

She was divorced, later becoming Tegwen Matthews when she married

Dr Peter Matthews, and her links with golf were only as a social player – until 2005 that was.

'I'd been asked a few times about getting involved with the WLGU but I've never been someone who wanted to sit on committees or get involved in administrative work. That just isn't me. Then Jill Edwards, who I'd known for many years, phoned me and her first words were: "Don't say no until you hear what I've got to say."'

'She wanted me to become Welsh captain and sold it to me on the basis there would only be a couple of weeks' commitment a year and I'd have a team manager to help me out.

'I was able to fit things in with my work schedule so I agreed and, although I was nervous when I first met these 16-19 year-old girls whose names I had only read about in the papers, it has been fantastic. My father was always keen for me to give something back to the sport and it's a shame he died before he was able to see me captaining Wales.'

And the Tegwen Matthews story came full circle in 2006 when she received a phone call from McKenna.

'Mary told me the LGU had asked her to captain the 2007 Vagliano Trophy and 2008 Curtis Cup teams but there was one thing preventing her from taking it. Then she told me that one thing was that I had to be her team manager. How could I refuse? It seemed so strange to be sorting out uniforms for the team all those years after I was being measured for my own Curtis Cup outfits.'

What made things extra special was the fact that the 2008 Curtis Cup was played for the first time at the Home of Golf, the Old Course at St Andrews and was also played over three days for the first time. Although GB&I were beaten 13-7, the new format proved to be a major success and for Matthews it was a thrill to be involved.

'To be team manager with the matches at St Andrews was a huge honour and maybe, just maybe, if we had won I might have decided to hang up my golf bag and look back on some wonderful memories.'

But the footnote to that was McKenna being asked to stay on as captain for the 2010 Curtis Cup at the Essex County Club in Boston, Massachusetts – with Matthews as her team manager.

The story goes on...

# Chapter Eleven
# Ian Woosnam

GOLFERS the world over have been faced with the scenario: a putt on the final green to win a Major.

All but the chosen few then wake up and reality dawns. But on Sunday, April 15, 1991, Ian Woosnam was not dreaming. The setting was the Augusta National in Georgia and his eight-footer was for the Masters title and the coveted green jacket. A few had gone close, but no Welshman had ever been able to proclaim himself a Major champion.

Woosnam arrived at the final tee 11 under-par and tied for the lead with his playing partner Tom Watson and with Jose Maria Olazabal. In the penultimate match up ahead, Spaniard Olazabal made bogey to drop to 10 under and all eyes were on Woosnam and Watson.

The American, one of the all-time greats of the sport, had been there many times before. He had eight Majors under his belt including two green jackets from his Masters wins. Woosnam, the 33-year-old pocket dynamite from Oswestry, had recently become the world number one – but this was an altogether different prospect. History shows that Watson double-bogeyed the last to drop to tied third while Woosnam was eight-feet from the flag in three, and needed to hole the par putt to join one of golf's most exclusive clubs.

'I'd watched that scene of making the winning putt on the 18th at The Masters so many times. But never did I feel I would have such a part to play in it. It was a nice putt. I aimed it at the right lip and told myself this was the time to keep my head down, stay calm and complete the stroke. It worked.'

That calm was soon overtaken as long-time caddie and close friend Phil Morbey, or 'Wobbly' as he is universally known, ran across and hoisted his employer into the air in celebration.

Fast forward a decade-and-a-half and Woosnam, less than two years away from joining the Seniors' Tour, stood on the balcony at the K Club, Ireland, doused in champagne and Guinness after captaining Europe to a record-equalling 18½-9½ Ryder Cup win against the United States. The images of the diminutive Welshman holding aloft the arm of big Irishman Darren Clarke, still grieving over the death of his wife Heather through cancer, will live forever and a day.

'The pinnacle of my career,' is how Woosnam described it. Some statement given all that he had achieved beforehand. The farmer's boy from Shropshire had done good. No doubt about that.

Woosnam landing at Cardiff airport after skippering
the victorious 2006 European Ryder Cup team

Woosnam with his home crowd in full support at the Epson Grand Prix of Europe at St Pierre

*(Media Wales)*

Ian Harold Woosnam was born in Oswestry on the Welsh-English border in March 1958, his family living in the nearby village of St Martin's. His first flirtation with golf came with Sunday afternoon visits to Llanymynech golf club, which has the distinction of being located both in Wales and England. Father Harold, the important business of the dairy farm done, transported the family the fourteen miles to Llanymynech, where a Welsh golfing legend was moulded.

Woosnam junior acquired his own custom set of cut-down clubs at the age of eight and there was no stopping him, those weekly visits becoming ever more frequent, especially during school holidays. By the age of twelve, Woosnam's handicap was 13, three years later and it was down to just 1, and the feisty temperament that would become a trademark was already evident as he refused to accept being anything other than the best. And at the age of thirteen, Woosnam won the Shropshire Junior Championship at The Wrekin and became a regular on the local circuit.

Although born on the 'wrong' side of the border, Woosnam always considered himself Welsh, with a strong Welsh family, so when it came to deciding international allegiance there was only one choice he was going to make. So selection for the North Wales Boys was followed by junior international honours as captain of the Welsh Boys and Woosnam reached the quarter-finals of the British Boys' Championship.

His senior debut for Wales came at the age of eighteen when he played in an international against France at Royal Porthcawl, but hopes of a first cap in the Home Internationals later that year were thwarted due to glandular fever.

Woosnam, who had left school at 16 with no academic qualifications, turned pro at the end of 1976, having spent two years as an assistant at the Hill Valley club. His move came one year ahead of his great rival in county competitions, Sandy Lyle. But, whereas Lyle enjoyed a fast-track transition from amateur to European Tour number one in the space of just over two years, Woosnam's bedding-in period was considerably longer and considerably tougher.

For five years Woosnam drove around Europe in his Volkswagen Dormobile in a fruitless quest to make a breakthrough, the 5ft 4in fighter earning less than £5,000 during those early barren years.

'In 1981 I was at Princes trying to qualify for the Open Championship at Royal St George's. I shot 67 on the first day but then hit it out of bounds on the 11th hole of my second round after a double bogey at the 10th. I walked off the course and drove all the way home to Shropshire vowing I would never play golf again.

'It took me a few weeks to calm down and then my parents persuaded me to go on as I hadn't yet given myself five years.'

In 1982 Woosnam's patience and persistence finally started to be rewarded with some decent finishes and, more importantly, some decent cheques. European Tour title number one came in the Ebel Swiss Open at Crans Sur Sierre in 1982, Woosnam losing a four-shot lead at the start of the final round before defeating Scot Bill Longmuir in a play-off. He celebrated with a few pints and a cigarette, before returning home more than £10,000 better off. And with the Dormobile a thing of the past Woosnam took receipt of a brand new Ford Escort RS2000.

From 104th on the Order of Merit in 1981, Woosnam leapt to 8th in 1982 with prize money in excess of £48,000. For fourteen of the next fifteen years, he would not drop out of the top dozen on the money list.

1983 saw Woosnam claim the Silk Cut Masters in front of his own Welsh supporters at St Pierre, and he was selected for Tony Jacklin's European team to face the USA in the Ryder Cup at Palm Beach Gardens, Florida.

Jack Nicklaus's Americans edged it 14½-13½, and the debutant Woosnam began his Ryder Cup career with a half in the fourballs with Sam Torrance against Calvin Peete and Ben Crenshaw in what would be the first of eight successive Ryder Cup appearances for Woosnam, as he became a linchpin of the European side during a golden age of matches on both sides of the pond.

In Europe's memorable 16½-11½ win at The Belfry in 1985, Woosnam contributed two points in tandem with Paul Way, and in the historic 15-13 success on US soil at Muirfield Village, Ohio in 1987, he and Nick Faldo were unbeaten in

Woosnam and caddie Phil Morbey at the 1993 Ryder Cup

*(Huw Evans Agency)*

the foursomes and fourballs, with three wins and a half. And that same Woosnam/Faldo combination was used to great effect again in the 14-14 tie at The Belfry in 1989, Europe retaining the cup as the holders.

After three successive victories Woosnam was on the losing side in 1991 – 'The War on the Shore' – at Kiawah Island, and in 1993 at The Belfry.

In the second of those defeats Woosnam enjoyed his finest Ryder Cup with two victories alongside Peter Baker, and two more alongside Bernhard Langer, before a half against Fred Couples on the final day. He became the first European to register a maximum haul in foursomes and fourballs.

Another nail-biting halved singles with Couples was Woosnam's key contribution to Europe's 14½-13½ victory at Oak Hill, New York, in 1995 and although not at his best when the same score was repeated at Valderrama in 1997, the Welshman still played his part.

During his Ryder Cup years Woosnam became one of the most instantly recognisable figures in world golf and the little Welshman with the big game was a crowd pleaser the world over.

Victories in the Scandinavian Open in 1984 and the Lawrence Batley International in 1985 cemented his position in Europe's top tier, and in 1987 Woosnam won four Tour titles and the World Matchplay at Wentworth for the first time – beating Lyle at the last hole in the final – on his way to becoming Europe's number one.

The icing on the cake to a glorious year came in Hawaii where Woosnam and David Llewellyn defeated Scotland's Lyle and Sam Torrance in a play-off to claim the World Cup of Golf. Fiercely patriotic, it still stands as one of the highlights of his career.

'Playing for Wales in the World Cup and Dunhill Cup was always a huge honour and to win with David in 1987 was fantastic. The final day brought gale force winds and torrential rain so the Welsh and the Scots felt at home!

'At the time Wales had just four players on Tour so it was almost unbelievable that we could win a World Cup.'

Woosie brought an even broader smile to his bank manager's face by landing the controversial Million Dollar Challenge in Sun City, a trip which earned him a place on the United Nations sporting blacklist as South Africa was still operating under the Apartheid regime.

Three more Tour victories followed in 1988, including the PGA Championship, and closer to home Woosnam earned a far more modest cheque for winning the Welsh Pros title.

After a relatively quiet 1989, there were four European Tour wins in 1990 plus a second World Matchplay as Woosnam was again crowned Europe's number one golfer.

The Masters triumph in 1991 was preceded three weeks earlier by Woosnam's maiden victory on the USPGA Tour in the USF&G Classic in New Orleans, and he returned home to capture another two European Tour titles including the second of three successive wins in the gamblers' paradise of Monte Carlo.

The Augusta win will never be forgotten but for Woosnam, the New Orleans success was also hugely significant as, 24 hours after lifting the trophy, the latest World Golf Rankings showed the Welshman at number one for the first time.

He would stay there for the next 50 weeks,

Woosnam and wife Glendryth after he was named 1991 Welsh Sports Personality of the Year, for the third time, following his Masters success

*(Media Wales)*

underlining his position as Wales's most successful sportsman of the modern era. Between 1986 and 1997 only once – in 1995 – did Woosnam fail to win a European Tour event, and his golden era concluded with four victories in 1996 and another PGA Championship the following year.

Even in his glory years, however, Woosnam was plagued by back problems and was diagnosed with ankylosing spondylitis, a condition that results in inflammation of the vertebrae.

Woosnam's playing appearances were reduced as the new millennium beckoned, and it was in May 2001 that his fourteen-year association with Morbey finally came to an end. Woosnam felt that 'Wobbly' was too good a caddy to be on the bag of a player who would not be in action as regularly as he had been used to, and urged him to go off and find another paymaster. Shortly after he was snapped up by Jose-Maria Olazabal, and Woosnam acquired a new bag man, 33-year-old Irishman Miles Byrne, who came from a family of caddies.

Byrne was to gain notoriety within a few months as he made the error which ultimately cost Woosnam the opportunity to add a second Major to his CV in the Open Championship at Royal Lytham & St Annes.

A resurgent Woosie went into the final round tied for the lead with German pair Alex Cejka and Bernhard Langer and American David Duval. And when he put his tee shot at the par-three opening hole to within four inches for a birdie start, Woosnam was leading the Championship and flying. Then, in an unforgettable moment, Byrne raised his palms in the air on the second tee and uttered the words: 'Boss, you're going to go ballistic.'

Woosnam had been testing a new driver on the range before the final round and Byrne had left it, along with his original, in the bag, making fifteen clubs and incurring a two-shot penalty.

It was a blow from which Woosnam never recovered and he eventually finished tied third behind Duval, his best Open placing since a third place in 1986 at Turnberry. Woosnam will also look back on his tie for second place behind Curtis Strange in the 1989 US Open at Oak Hill, New York as another near miss in a Major. Ironically Strange was in the commentary box for US television network ABC and called the fifteenth club incident in 2001.

From the nightmare of Lytham, Woosnam went on to beat Padraig Harrington in the final of the World Matchplay at Wentworth that autumn, making him the first player to win the title in three different decades. But that was Woosnam's last significant win of a professional career on the main Tour that saw him capture 28 European titles, two PGA Tour wins and 14 other titles around the globe. And in addition to his eight Ryder Cup appearances, Woosnam represented Wales nine times in the Dunhill Cup and 15 times in the World Cup.

That team ethic led to his appointment as an assistant to Sam Torrance on the 2002 winning European Ryder Cup side and his own glory run as captain in 2006. Woosnam's 1991 triumph at Augusta saw him crowned Welsh Sports Personality of the Year – one of three times he picked up the award – and his list of achievements in professional sport is unrivalled among his countrymen and women.

Another of his great passions has been snooker and Woosnam served a term as Chairman of the World Professional Billiards and Snooker Association.

Based for many years in Jersey with wife Glendryth and their three children, Woosnam has continued to play selected European Tour events and, after being awarded the OBE in the 2007 New Years Honours, he started looking forward to the next chapter of his career in Seniors' golf.

He turned 50 in March 2008 and had to battle his way through a period of ill health ahead of his latest challenge.

'Reaching 50 is a significant milestone in anyone's life, but for a golfer, to be able to start again among so many old friends and world-class players is a great honour and it was one that I was looking forward to.'

Woosnam gets in some putting practice ahead of his opening round in the 2002 Wales Open at Celtic Manor
*(Media Wales)*

It came as little surprise to anyone that Woosnam's bedding-in period on the Seniors' Tour was an altogether more comfortable affair than he had gone through on the main tour all those years earlier. His first season on the Over-50s tour produced victories in the 2008 Russian and Polish Senior Opens and it set Woosnam up to win the coveted John Jacobs Trophy for the Order of Merit winner. That made him the first player to top the money lists on both the main and Seniors' Tours.

In 2009 he only just missed out on retaining his crown when old pal Sam Torrance nudged him into second place on the Order of Merit in the final tournament.

Given his standing in Wales, Woosnam has inevitably had to face a barrage of questions as to his possible involvement in the 2010 Ryder Cup. No doubt he will receive the hero's welcome he deserves at Celtic Manor, but Woosnam is adamant his role will be that of partisan supporter and nothing else.

'I've done my bit and I don't need to do it again,' he reflected. 'It's time for others to take over. It's going to be a fantastic spectacle and nothing will stop me being there, but only as a spectator.

'Many sceptics thought they would never see the day when the Ryder Cup came to Wales. I was never one of those and I believe we will put on an event that the country will forever be proud of.'

In an era where professional golfers spend as much time in the gym as on the golf course, Woosnam is probably an endangered species –

and the game will be worse for it when he, and some of his contemporaries, call time on their careers. Indeed, Woosnam once said that his popularity worldwide was down to the fact that he was the antithesis of the six-foot, six-pack athlete, an ordinary bloke who loves playing golf but also loves a pint and a cigarette. Ordinary bloke maybe, but no ordinary golfer. Quite simply the greatest Wales has produced.

Woosnam with the legendary American course designer Robert Trent Jones Snr at the opening of Celtic Manor's Roman Road course in 1995
*(Media Wales)*

Phil Parkin

# Chapter Twelve

# Phil Parkin

AMID the blooming azaleas in the Augusta springtime, a 22-year-old amateur would normally be anonymous as the giants of world golf prepare for the US Masters.

But in 1984, a young Welshman by the name of Phil Parkin caused quite a stir and captured the imagination not just of the famous Augusta galleries, but of the great Jack Nicklaus as well.

Parkin was at Augusta by invitation after his victory in the Amateur Championship the previous year and was standing on the practice range the day before his opening round, when he would partner the legendary Arnold Palmer. The 290-yard range had a 40-foot high net fence at the end of it and news quickly spread among the crowd of the amateur who was hitting the ball a country mile.

'I was so pumped by the whole Augusta experience that I was hitting the ball over the fence and the crowd were going wild,' recalled Parkin. 'Then Jack Nicklaus wandered down from the other end of the range and started to watch me for a while. I hit a few more big ones and then he called Lanny Wadkins and Tom Weiskopf over to have a look.

'Nicklaus then took me back another 20 yards to a gap between the stands where there was barely enough room to swing a club. He said: "Let's see you hit it over the fence now hotshot." And I did!'

When it came to the first round of the tournament, Parkin's drive at the opening hole got to within 30 yards of the green, a distance which had never been witnessed at Augusta and one which wouldn't be seen again until Tiger Woods emerged on the scene.

With the course lengthened extensively in recent years, no one, not even Woods, has managed to get closer to the first green.

Parkin narrowly missed the cut, but had carved his name into Masters folklore, and plenty of informed pundits were backing him to become one of the great names in British and European golf.

Born in Doncaster in 1962, Andrew Philip Parkin moved to the mid-Wales market town of Newtown at the age of five and took up golf at the tiny St Giles club, with its nine holes nestling alongside the River Severn. Parkin, who attended Newtown High School, started off with a handicap of 40 but was dedicated to his endless practice sessions and by the age of 16 had reduced it to just two under the guidance of Sid Collins, the club professional.

He had won a couple of Mid-Wales Boys' titles but his first major breakthrough

Amateur champion Parkin at the Masters at Augusta in 1984 with the legendary Arnold Palmer in the background    *(Media Wales)*

came in 1982 when he spread-eagled the field at St Andrews to capture the British Youths' Championship by seven shots.

His coach David Clay, a former teaching professional in Portugal who relocated to Newtown as a director of the Petron golf clubs manufacturing company, then paved the way for Parkin, who was working full-time in an accounts office, to start a scholarship at Texas A&M University near Houston, where he would combine his golf with a business degree. Parkin had attended clinics held by the esteemed US golf guru Gary Wiren and from there he found himself heading across the pond.

During his college years Parkin progressed to the lofty heights of a place in the coveted All American first team, and the experience of flying all over the States gave him an early taste of the existence of a tour player.

'I was the first overseas player to be named as a first team All American and I was regularly beating the likes of Colin Montgomerie, Steve Elkington, Davis Love III and Scott Verplank. People will think I'm mad for saying it, but at that time golf was just so easy for me.'

So easy, in fact, that Parkin actually set himself some unbelievable challenges just to stretch himself.

'I remember playing in one college event in Athens, Georgia, and I decided not to use any wooden clubs throughout the whole round, only my irons. Then I decided

Parkin, left, after beating Ian Woosnam, right, to win the
1986 Welsh Professional Championship at Whitchurch
*(Media Wales)*

not to use any of my wedges either. I finished one shot out of the lead and had it not been for a guy holing an outrageous putt at the last, I would have won.'

It was on one of his trips home from America in the summer of 1983 that Parkin made everyone stand up and take notice as he won the Amateur Championship over the Turnberry links. He actually led the qualifiers from the 36 holes of strokeplay despite signing for a wrong score in the second round and being forced to take one stroke too many. And in the matchplay stages, he was never taken the distance and swept aside American Walker Cup player Jim Holtgrieve 5&4.

In the Welsh Amateur Championship at Southerndown, Parkin just failed to complete the double as the experienced John Roger Jones defeated him at the last hole of a thrilling final. Both those performances came on the back of a Walker Cup debut, Parkin winning two of his three matches in Great Britain and Ireland's 13½-10½ defeat against the Americans over the Royal Liverpool links at Hoylake.

Parkin's first appearance in the Open Championship at Royal Birkdale pushed him firmly into the spotlight again, and after a superb opening round of 69 he was on course to make the cut, only to miss out by one stroke after a 78 on the second day.

Following his Masters experience in the spring of 1984, Parkin retained his GB&I place for the St Andrews Trophy match against the Rest of Europe at Saunton. It said much for his reputation that the whole match was being billed as a head-to-head between Parkin for GB&I and a young Spaniard – Jose Maria Olazabal – for Europe.

He then set about defending the Amateur Championship at Formby. Just as he had twelve months earlier, Parkin led the strokeplay qualifying competition.

'In the week before the Amateur I played at Formby with Colin Montgomerie and I shot 62. He told me that there was no point anyone else turning up if I played like that.'

Montgomerie would later describe Parkin as the best amateur player he had ever seen. Disappointingly he only reached the last 16 of the matchplay before losing 4&2 to Scottish teenager Colin Brooks, and that defeat prompted the announcement that many had been expecting at some point during the year. Parkin was to turn professional.

Given his profile and status it was no surprise that Parkin's professional debut would come in the biggest tournament of them all, the Open Championship at St Andrews. Never one to do anything by halves, Parkin, after three successive rounds of 73 on the Old Course, closed out the tournament with a 69 to tie 31st place alongside such luminaries as Nicklaus and Johnny Miller.

Of more significance was the steely determination Parkin showed on the final green, holing a 35-foot birdie putt which saw him finish level par for the tournament and bank a cheque for just over £2,000, an amount that immediately earned him a European Players' card.

With his season only starting in July, Parkin went on to amass over £11,500 during the remainder of the campaign, making 11 straight cuts, finishing 65th on the Order of Merit, claiming the Sir Henry Cotton Rookie of the Year award and making his World Cup debut for Wales. Indeed, Cotton himself increased the speed of the Parkin bandwagon by declaring there was no reason why the Welshman could not go on to earn a place in the European Ryder Cup team for the 1985 matches at The Belfry.

He just missed out on the team despite finishing inside the top 40 on the Order of Merit in 1985 (as he would again in 1986). And he failed to get that all-important first Tour win, runners-up spot in Jersey in 1985 his best finish.

Parkin returned to Wales to win the Welsh PGA title at Whitchurch in 1986, producing two stunning rounds of 65 to finish four strokes clear of his nearest challenger, Ian Woosnam.

Still regarded as the greatest unfulfilled talent in British golf, Parkin headed back to the United States and finished third in the notoriously tough qualifying school to earn a PGA Tour card for 1987. But far from solving all of his problems, it merely added to them.

At the age of 25 Parkin should have had the world at his feet, but ultimately paid the price for spreading himself too thinly trying to keep up with his commitments on both sides of the Atlantic.

'I made the mistake of trying to play in my favourite tournaments on both Tours and got into a situation where I would play a couple of US events then dash back to Europe for a couple. With all the travelling and the associated jet-lag there was no chance for me to settle and play the golf I was capable of in America or Europe.

'In the States they had a re-rank after everyone had played in three events, and I found myself going backwards at a rate of knots. You need to be playing continually to give yourself a chance and I didn't do that, and paid the penalty. My game suffered badly and my confidence dropped dramatically. It was a bit of a disaster.'

Parkin's PGA Tour nightmare is perhaps summed up by the story of him arriving by plane into Providence, Rhode Island, for the Providence Classic – or so he thought.

Baffled by the lack of any greeters or courtesy cars at the airport Parkin made a telephone call to a friend and, after checking the schedule, discovered that he should have been heading for the Provident Classic in Chattanooga, Tennessee.

He jumped back on a plane and arrived at the right destination on the Wednesday night, had to tee off early on the Thursday morning and, not surprisingly, missed the cut.

The American dream had turned into something of a nightmare for Parkin and his career never really recovered from it.

He continued to play in Europe and briefly, with a second place finish in the Majorcan Open in 1989, threatened to make the impact that everyone had anticipated

Parkin on duty for the BBC during the Open championship    (Media Wales)

a few years earlier. But major success eluded him and a constant battle with eye problems further eroded his confidence and ability to play at the top level.

As far back as 1988 Parkin had been to an eye specialist and wore corrective spectacles for two hours every day over a period of two years to try and cure the problem.

'If I hadn't been a professional golfer my eyesight would have been good enough to get by, but you have to be able to read the subtleties of the greens and I couldn't do that. It got so bad that, at times, I would spend the practice days at tournaments just mapping out the greens and trying to remember the breaks because I knew I wouldn't be able to read them. Looking back I'm amazed I could even contend for so many tournaments given how bad my putting was. Unless I hit my irons to within a couple of feet of the flag I didn't have a chance.'

Parkin even turned to a ground-breaking Russian eye-hospital ship in Dubai in 1996, but it was several years later, with his tournament career ended, that he found the answers he was looking for in the Johns Hopkins Hospital, Baltimore.

'Dr David Guyton, at the Wilmer Eye Institute, discovered that my left eye was tilting, which meant I was seeing everything at an angle. Worse still, depending on how tired my eyes were, the degree of that angle would get steeper so I could be seeing the same putt three different ways at three different times of day. The bottom line was that I never really had a chance to win tournaments because of it.'

His European Tour career came to an end in 1992, a year in which he was famously disqualified from the Italian Open after finding an illegal extra club – his two-year-old son's toy putter – at the bottom of his bag.

His tournament career over, Parkin was able to maintain an interest in the game as an on-course commentator and analyst with Sky Sports, travelling the world as part of their European Tour broadcasting team from 1994. He quickly became one of the most likeable and intelligent analysts in the sport, and was also on hand to be able to pass on some useful advice to the Tour players.

'While I was commentating I'd get a few requests from some of the players to take a look at their game, especially the short game and putting. I even helped out Colin Montgomerie and Phil Price on occasions.

It was that instinctive ability to coach, and an interest in further developing that string to his bow, which saw Parkin move back to the States in 2004 to take up a post at the prestigious David Leadbetter Academy in Bradenton, Florida.

'Obviously America appealed to me, especially the climate, and it was a chance to develop the interest in coaching that I'd had for a long time.'

The likes of Paula Creamer, who has since gone on to become a sensation on the

LPGA Tour, emerged through the Leadbetter Academy ranks and Parkin relished his time working with the superstars of tomorrow.

Back in Europe, Parkin has most recently been picking up his broadcasting career with both the BBC and was a regular studio analyst for Setanta Sports. And as part of the BBC's award-winning golf team, Parkin's calm and authoritative voice is now instantly recognisable to millions of fans.

Parkin still has his home in Florida, where he counts victorious 2008 US Ryder Cup skipper Paul Azinger and former European captain and double Major-winner Tony Jacklin among his neighbours. Now aged 48, and with some corrective surgery carried out on his eyes, it remains to be seen whether Parkin will try again to make his impact as a tournament player in Seniors' golf when he passes 50.

'I'm still not sure I would be able to read greens well enough to really compete but maybe I'll give it a go when the time comes, you never say never. I just wish I could have had three or four years on Tour with good eyesight, because I know I would have won a lot of tournaments.'

There is no doubt that his massive potential was never fully realised, but Phil Parkin provided plenty of memorable moments during a rollercoaster ride.

A teenage Phil Parkin making his mark in Welsh amateur golf

# Chapter Thirteen

# Paul Mayo

WHAT do you do when you are potentially good enough to make an impact at rugby and football? In the case of Paul Mayo the answer was to give up both and start playing golf.

And what a decision that proved to be as Mayo became one of the most decorated amateurs in Welsh golfing history before going on to forge a successful career as a Tour, and then a club, professional.

In 1987 Mayo enjoyed the sort of run most sportsmen can only dream about, winning the Amateur Championship, the Welsh Championship, the Silver Medal at The Open and appearing in the Walker Cup in the space of a few months. It was a sequence the like of which has rarely been seen in such a competitive sport.

A standout sportsman at St Julian's school, Newport, Mayo, born in the town in 1963, was already making waves in both codes of football before taking the decision that would set him on the road to glory.

'I was captain of the school team at rugby, football, cricket and baseball, and I played for the county schools at football and rugby,' recalled Mayo. 'It got to a stage where my rugby coach took me to one side and told me I had a chance to make it, but I'd have to give up soccer and concentrate all my energies on the one sport. Then I went to see my soccer coach and he told me exactly the same, that a few clubs were showing an interest in me and I could take it further.'

Mayo, a scrum-half of obvious potential, was playing inside Stuart Barnes for the county schools. Barnes went on to win ten caps for England and is now one of the game's most respected writers and broadcasters.

But for Mayo the solution to his problem was a radical one.

'My mother and father had both been captains at Llanwern Golf Club and my three brothers were all playing golf. So one day I went home, told my father I was packing in rugby and football and that I was going to play golf too. Once I'd started, my handicap came down pretty quickly and by early 1979, I was playing off 2.'

Mayo was to win the Welsh Boys' Championship later that year and his rapid development was nurtured by Llanwern professional Graham Poor, who would become the head professional at Royal Porthcawl until his tragic death in an air crash in Italy in 1993. Mayo has always held him in the very highest regard and was one of the driving forces behind the introduction of the Graham Poor South Wales PGA Memorial Matchplay, which is contested each year.

With his victory in the Welsh Boys and international honours at junior level, the

91

Mayo acknowledges the gallery after winning the Welsh Professional
Championship at Fairwood Park in 1991          (*Media Wales*)

young Mayo, now a member at Newport, quickly acquired a taste for success and his sights were very firmly trained on making a career for himself in golf. And on his travels to the various tournaments around the country, Mayo forged a friendship with Philip Parkin, a player in whose footsteps he would follow as Amateur Champion and as a golf scholar in the United States.

'Phil was from Newtown but he was working with a very good coach there by the name of David Clay. David was making some inroads into setting up a few scholarships to America, and Phil was starting at Texas A&M University near Houston,' said Mayo. 'I started working with David and, after I finished my junior career in 1981 and sat my exams, I was planning to take a gap year to do some travelling and play more golf.

'Phil had been in the States for one semester and I was offered a place there myself. I didn't really know anything about the place, and I went over sight unseen, but in January 1982 I was officially a student there.'

For the next few years Mayo would combine his golf with a degree in business management, minoring in psychology, two subjects that would be of use as his career progressed on and off the course.

'The general misconception about college in America is that you just play your sport for four or five years and then they hand you a degree at the end of it. The bottom line is that you have to keep your study grades to a required level and to combine that with sport takes a lot of dedication. I suppose I was fortunate to have been brought up in a family where the work ethic was instilled in me, and that certainly helped me a great deal when I was in Texas.'

As for his golf, that improved steadily as he travelled the college circuit rubbing shoulders with the likes of Scott Verplank, Jeff Maggert, Billy Andrade, Steve Elkington and Davis Love III, players who would all become household names on the PGA Tour.

'It's a bit of a cliché but it did change my life. I hadn't travelled that far and I certainly hadn't gained too much life experience, so it was something that stood me in good stead for becoming a Tour professional.'

Having won the British Youths' Championship in 1983, Mayo played in the first of his two Walker Cups in 1985 at Pine Valley, partnering Colin Montgomerie to a memorable half in their foursomes against the top US pairing of Verplank and Jay Sigel.

He graduated in 1987 and returned home for the summer to capture the Welsh title and the Amateur Championship at Prestwick, defeating one of the great amateurs of the modern era, Peter McEvoy, in the final. That success came just a week after he had been controversially left out of both sets of singles by captain Geoff Marks in

GB&I's heavy Walker Cup defeat at Sunningdale.

'My abiding memory of the whole week is my dad Roy charging onto the green after I holed the winning putt on the 17th and shouting 'We're going to the Masters'.

'Up to then I had just been concentrating on each match and I knew I was playing pretty well but I hadn't really thought about the implications of winning. Afterwards it started to dawn on me that I was the Amateur Champion, and I would be playing in the Open and the Masters at Augusta.'

Prestwick, venue for the very first Open Championship in 1860, has remained close to Mayo's heart and he still finds time to fit in a couple of visits to the famous old links every year.

A fresh-faced Mayo reads a putt while caddying for brother Chris in 1980                    *(Media Wales)*

The first of his invitations as Amateur Champion was to the 1987 Open at Muirfield, where Nick Faldo would claim the first of his three Claret Jugs.

'I was paired with Jeff Hawkes and Mark Calcavecchia (who would become Open champion two years later at Troon) for the first two rounds, and on the first tee I was just thinking that I shouldn't be here. I was this skinny 24-year-old amateur playing in The Open with the greatest names in golf.'

As it turned out, Mayo acquitted himself superbly, making the halfway cut and actually seeing his name on the leaderboard – albeit fleetingly.

'I got to the par three 13th, on the second day, and I was one under for the tournament. From the tee I could see the scoreboard at the back of the green and there was the name … MAYO.

'Then I dumped my tee shot into the bunker where it plugged, took two to get out and made double bogey. As I was walking off the green they were taking my name off the board.'

By Sunday Mayo was assured of the Silver Medal for the leading amateur, but had to contend with some of the worst final round weather the Open has ever seen.

93

'I was paired with Fuzzy Zoeller, who had a reputation for being one of the quickest players around. When I went into the locker room I saw Zoeller and Lee Trevino sitting down chatting and looking out of the big window at the conditions. I thought I'd better go and introduce myself, after which Zoeller looked me up and down and said: "I hope you've got your tennis shoes on boy, because we ain't gonna be hanging around out there today."'

The experience of The Open and the Walker Cup proved invaluable as Mayo then headed to Augusta in the spring of 1988 to take up his Masters invitation.

'It was a very special week. I had my father on the bag and we were playing with the great Jack Nicklaus in the first round: it doesn't get much better than that. I was never going to do much and making the cut would have been my only realistic aim. But I remember after the second round, I was interviewed by Steve Rider on BBC and I announced that I would be turning professional. I even stayed on to do some commentary and actually called a few shots from Sandy Lyle, who went on to win the green jacket that year.'

There was little time to bask in the glories of his amateur career as Mayo headed straight for the European Tour qualifying school at La Manga, where he secured his card with a tied-second finish alongside Vijay Singh and Jesper Parnevik, Englishman Russell Claydon the only player ahead of them.

Mayo was to spend the next seven years on Tour without ever achieving the same level of success he did as an amateur. Sixth place was his highest finish and a back injury sustained when lifting a suitcase out of a car in Jersey plagued him for several years.

However, he has absolutely no regrets and argues that 'achievements' can be measured in many different ways.

'I never won a European Tour event but I won plenty of other tournaments, played for Wales in the Dunhill Cup and made a decent living. Everything I have is my own and so who can say that I wasn't successful?'

Mayo won two Welsh Professional Championships in 1991 and 1992, played in The Open in 1989, 1990, 1991, 1992 and 1995, claimed a PGA Assistants' Championship and represented Wales twice in the European Club Pros' Championship. It was at The Open in 1995 at St Andrews that Mayo decided he would leave the Tour at the end of that season, a decision which surprised many.

'I was actually playing quite well at the time but I saw a few of the older guys on Tour who were struggling with their next move and I knew that I didn't want to be in that situation. The European Tour was also moving into South Africa and the Far East and with a one-year-old son the prospect of packing my bags for weeks at a time was losing its appeal.

'I would never give it less than 100 per cent and I didn't think I could do that anymore so I told my wife Hazel and then had to tell my father, which I was dreading. He had been my right hand man, my caddie, my chauffeur, pretty much everything. But, as he always had, he backed my decision and told me to move on to the next stage of my life.'

As Mayo had already qualified as a PGA professional while on Tour, that next stage would be as a club pro, and where better than at Newport?

'Roy Skuse was the pro at the time and he had been suffering from ill health and would be retiring when his contract was up, so I put in an application. It wasn't cut and dried just because of my ties with the club. I had to go through the same process as everyone else.'

He was selected for the post and has remained there to this day, forging a reputation not just as a first-class head pro, but also as a coach. He worked with Bradley Dredge for six years and now does valuable work with some of Gwent's top juniors. He also takes great pleasure in seeing his two sons Josh and Scott enjoying the sport that has been his life.

'As a club professional I wouldn't want to be anywhere else. With the Ryder Cup coming to Newport in 2010, we are going to be firmly in the spotlight and this is an opportunity we can't afford to waste. And it's not just about 2010, but about 2020 and 2030. We need to create a legacy that will last for decades to come.'

Having achieved so much as a tournament player, Mayo inevitably gets asked whether or not he will try his hand at the Seniors' Tour when he becomes eligible. But the question always meets with the same response.

'I'm just past my mid forties and I get people asking me about the Seniors' Tour, what a cheek!'

If he never plays another tournament in his life Mayo has more than enough happy memories to draw on. And if Wales ever produces a more successful amateur then he will have to be some player.

Mayo putting during the Welsh
professional championship
*(Media Wales)*

Phillip Price

# Chapter Fourteen
# Phillip Price

WHEN the normally placid and mild-mannered Phillip Price clenched his fist and gritted his teeth on the 16th green at The Belfry after defeating world number two Phil Mickelson in the 2002 Ryder Cup, it was the defining moment of a remarkable transition from ordinary Joe to national hero.

For a long time Price had been, in his own words, 'just a middle-of-the-road golfer', but his achievements are testament to the old ethos of hard work and dedication eventually reaping their rewards.

He may not have been blessed with the natural talents of the American whose colours he so memorably lowered on that autumnal Sunday afternoon, but the record books show the Newport-based Price has earned his place among the very highest echelons of the Welsh game.

Dedication is perhaps the word best used to describe Price, whose journey to the upper reaches of the sport has not been without its setbacks. Born in Pontypridd in 1966, just a decent long-iron down the hill from the town's golf club, Price was swinging a club in the family garden almost as soon as he could walk. His father and elder brothers were members of the club and he could hardly wait to follow in the family footsteps. Ironically, by the time he was enrolled as a junior member himself at the age of thirteen – a year after a trip to the Dunlop Masters at St Pierre, Chepstow had further whetted his appetite – his brothers' enthusiasm for the sport had waned.

Never academically gifted, sport, and golf in particular (although he did enjoy his outings as a flanker for the school rugby XV) was Price's preferred career choice from the outset. His early promise on the fairways and greens would no doubt have attracted attention from county and national coaching schemes a few years down the line, but Price recalls his development as being rather unorthodox.

'To be honest I didn't really have any structured coaching until I was about seventeen or eighteen,' he said. 'I was fortunate that Pontypridd had a very good team environment and some very good golfers, and it was playing with them that allowed me to improve. You could never say I was over-coached. Playing round after round was my learning curve.'

From the age of fifteen, Price had already made up his mind that he wanted to be a golf professional, and he took on a variety of jobs from leaflet distributor to shelf stacker in order to earn money that would allow him to compete on the amateur tournament circuit.

Price, on the eve of the Wales Open in 2006

*(Media Wales)*

Price celebrates with family and friends at Pontypridd golf club after his maiden European Tour win in the 1994 Portuguese Open                                                                 *(Media Wales)*

He played for Wales at Boys and Youths level, and represented the Great Britain and Ireland Boys before going on to win senior international honours for his country. But it was in the autumn of 1989 that Price eventually took the plunge and, with some sponsorship from a Pontypridd club member, relinquished his amateur status to pursue his dreams of becoming a pro.

'They were nervous times because that first season as a pro is massively tough. To be honest, I wasn't that good a player compared to some coming out of the amateur game, and if you don't get a Tour card straight away and start earning money then you are under a lot of pressure, especially financially.'

Price did manage to secure his European Tour card for 1990, but the withdrawal of his financial backing meant his plans could have been thwarted even before they began.

'My parents didn't have any more money to keep me going so it was a very uncertain period, but I guess a lot of players have to experience that at the start of their careers.'

Price did then what he has always done: got his head down, worked hard, pulled in the purse strings and started to appear on the European Tour radar. Between 1990 and 1994, when he won his first Tour title at the Algarve Portuguese Open, Price was very much in the journeyman category, winning enough money to keep himself in a relatively comfortable lifestyle but never really threatening to force his way to the top table.

'Even after that first win in Portugal, I felt that I was not really going where I wanted to go. I was starting to get a little fed up with being just another rank-and-file pro, and I knew I needed to do something or that was going to be where I stayed.'

What did happen is that Price met his wife Sandra, whom he credits with playing a key role in his quantum leap between 1998 and 2003.

'Sandra started to travel with me and all of a sudden, I was happy being away from home. The pressure of living out of a suitcase was eased, and any golfer will tell you if they are happy off the course then they achieve more on it. I made a massive leap forward from 1998 and my focus changed completely. I started looking more closely at my game, putting in more effort on the practice ground and made up my mind that I wanted to break out of the rut I had been in.'

Price was married in 1999 and his son John was born the following year, with daughter Hannah arriving in 2006.

His work with renowned sports psychologist Alan Fine was another contributory factor.

Price finished 15th on the Volvo Order of Merit in 1998, 36th in 1999 and a career-best eighth in 2000, when his earnings for the season broke through the million euro mark. With the Ryder Cup at The Belfry scheduled for September 2001, Price's memorable 2000 season, which included a tie for second behind Tiger Woods in the WGC NEC Invitational in Ohio, put him very much in contention for a place in Sam Torrance's European team.

In 2001 Price was just outside the top 20 on the Order of Merit but a second Tour win, again in Portugal, ensured that he gained the 10th and final automatic place in the European side.

Then came the terrorist attacks on the World Trade Center in New York and the subsequent postponement of the Ryder Cup matches until the following year. And that postponement was to have more implications for Price than most.

'It was bizarre because under normal circumstances you play your way into the Ryder Cup and then go straight into the matches, hopefully carrying your form with you. The 12 months between the original date and the rescheduled one seemed like a lifetime and, to be honest, it wasn't a great time for me.'

Price struggled to make the top 50 on the Order of Merit in 2002 and the decision to retain the same Ryder Cup teams from the aborted matches the previous year was to make him a scapegoat for the media, who were openly questioning his right to line up for Europe.

'I wasn't the only player, on both sides, whose form had dipped in the intervening twelve months but for some reason I got more stick that anyone else. Some of the comments in the media were out of order, and there were even some from certain players, which were quite hard to take.

'If the decision had been taken to pick new teams then I would have abided by it, but as far as I was concerned, I played my way in on merit and unless I was physically injured there was no way I was going to miss out on the chance to play in a Ryder Cup.

'I knew myself that I hadn't been playing well, but I also knew that I was capable of contributing to the team. The weeks leading up to it were horrible but once I got to The Belfry and started to practise I felt fine.'

Price, not totally unexpectedly for a rookie, was restricted to a watching brief during the Friday fourballs and foursomes, before making his debut on the Saturday alongside Sweden's Pierre Fulke.

They were beaten 2&1 by Mickelson and David Toms, and Price came out of the hat alongside Mickelson again, in the penultimate match, when the pairings were drawn for Sunday's decisive singles matches. On paper it was a banker point for the USA.

Price, inspired by the heroics of his team-mates elsewhere on the course, had other ideas. Every time Mickelson hit the ball close to the pin Price responded by hitting it even closer. His putting was also from the Gods that day, and by the time they reached the 16th the Welshman was two up and standing over a 25-foot putt for birdie. He holed it, as he had pretty much everything else on the day, Mickelson missed from 20-feet for a half, and the point was in the bag. Soon afterwards Irishman Paul McGinley closed out the victory for Europe.

'I'm not normally one to react with fist pumping and shouting but that day was just so different to anything I'd experienced before. I suppose there was an element of satisfaction at proving the critics wrong but the overwhelming emotion came from having made such a decisive contribution to the team.'

Now one of the leading lights on the European Tour, 2003 was another stellar year for Price as he gained his biggest tournament win yet in the European Open at the K Club, on his way to another million Euro season.

By that stage America was already on his mind, and Price was starting to formulate plans to further enhance his career on the other side of the Atlantic.

'I'd been playing between eight and ten events in America for a few years and had experience of the Majors and the World Championship events over there. But I didn't have a full Tour card, so I decided that for 2005 I would go through the qualifying school and have a crack at it. The qualifying system in the States is pretty long, pretty arduous and a lot of hassle, but I got my card and thought I was on my way.'

Unfortunately for Price he found out, like many others, that playing in the States is a whole new ball game.

'I didn't get as many starts as I thought I was going to early on and, without a permanent base, I was spending weeks in hotel rooms with nothing to do.'

By the time he established a permanent home in Florida and was joined by his family, Price was already struggling. A tie for 11th in the Fedex St Jude Classic was to be his best finish of a year that turned sour.

'I wish the transition had been a bit easier but it didn't work out and I never really settled in. I decided to stick it out for the whole season and I could have stayed for 2006 on a lower category exemption. But I had a good exemption in Europe and decided that it would be better to come home.

'It did turn a bit sour but I'm not sorry I went there. Hopefully the experience will stand me in good stead for playing tournament golf over there in future."

On his return to Wales Price slowly began to rebuild his standing on the European Tour and he remains as committed as ever to scaling the heights again, with the 2010 Ryder Cup in his own backyard at Celtic Manor an obvious target. Since 2006 Price has failed to break into the top 100 on the European Tour Order of Merit, and had to sit anxiously at home during the final event of 2009 – the new Dubai World Championships, to find out whether or not his playing rights for 2010 would be retained.

Having finished 198th on the OM and with his regular exemption expired, Price had to rely on his standing inside the top 40 all-time money winners in Europe to keep his full card. Several players in Dubai could have overhauled Price, but ironically only his fellow Welshman, Bradley Dredge, did so, knocking him from 38th to 39th on the list and so, by the skin of his teeth, ensuring another campaign in 2010.

Holding aloft the 2002 Ryder Cup trophy with Ian Woosnam                    *(Colorsport)*

101

'To play a Ryder Cup at home would be unbelievable and you never know what might happen,' said Price.

A proud Welshman who has represented his nation nine times in the World Cup and three times in the Dunhill Cup, Price is thrilled to see the game in Wales moving forward at such a pace.

'Given the size of our country, the number of players we have on the European Tour now is pretty impressive. The Golf Union of Wales deserves a huge amount of credit for putting in place the systems that have allowed so many good young players to come through.'

And pleased as he is to see the next generation of Dragons emerging, Price still harbours plenty of ambition of his own, and sees his future firmly ensconced in the sport that has been his life for the greater part of three decades.

'At the moment I don't see myself doing anything else. I love playing golf and as long as that continues, and I still have my health, I'm fairly certain that I'll carry on playing for as long as possible. I still have ambitions. I want to get back into the world's top-50 and win tournaments.'

Given his form of recent years, a playing resurgence to threaten Colin Montgomerie's 2010 European team would appear unlikely, but another possible avenue opened up for Price when Monty suggested his name as a possible vice-captain at the Celtic Manor.

'To even be considered by Monty as one of his back-room team is an honour and obviously, if the chance were to arise, I would relish playing a part in Wales's Ryder Cup.'

He has done it once. What Price for him to do it again?

Price hits his drive at the second hole in the 2002 Wales Open at Celtic Manor
*(Media Wales)*

Price in his early days as a professional playing in the Welsh Professional Championship at Mountain Lakes

*(Media Wales)*

Stephen Dodd

# Chapter Fifteen
# Stephen Dodd

AS an amateur, Stephen Dodd was used to being at the head of the field. As a professional, he wasn't exactly an overnight success.

But adopting the old adage 'If at first you don't succeed, try, try again', Dodd eventually fulfilled the promise he had shown during a distinguished amateur career to take his place at Europe's top table.

When the laid-back and quietly spoken Barry golfer arrived in Shanghai in late November 2004 – bizarrely for the first event of the 2005 European Tour season – he was, without any disrespect, an established journeyman. Since making his Tour debut as an amateur almost fifteen years earlier Dodd, at the age of 38, had appeared in 165 tournaments without a win. He had been through the annual torture of the tour qualifying school no less than ten times.

It was all a far cry from the heady heights of 1989 when Dodd became the first man ever to win the Welsh Matchplay, Strokeplay and British Amateur Championship titles in one season. There was also the small matter of being part of the first Great Britain and Ireland Walker Cup team to win on American soil at Peachtree, Atlanta.

So Dodd's three-shot victory ahead of the vastly experienced Danish Ryder Cup star Thomas Bjorn in the Volvo China Open might well have been greeted with all manner of bells and whistles. But Dodd, a modest and understated individual, was more a graduate of the Kipling school, treating triumph just as he had treated the odd disaster along the way.

'I thought that I would win a Tour event given time,' he reflected afterwards. 'Obviously it took a lot longer than I thought it would. But I never believed that I wasn't good enough. If I had thought like that I would have given up the Tour a long time before.'

That victory gave Dodd what every Tour professional craves. Not only was there the euphoria of victory and a cheque for almost £90,000 to keep the bank manager happy, but he left China clutching a two-year exemption.

Every player who wins on Tour for the first time will tell you that the exemption is key. It allows them to tailor their own schedule and relieves the continual pressure of playing week after week to earn enough money to guarantee playing rights for the next season. And for Dodd, just like London buses, you wait for one victory to come along and before you know it, there are three of them in the bank.

In the same 2005 season Dodd added the Nissan Irish Open title – and partnered

Stephen Dodd in action during the 2006 Welsh PGA Championship at Tenby

*(Media Wales)*

Bradley Dredge to the World Cup of Golf crown in Portugal – before adding his third Tour win in the European Open, again in Ireland, in 2006. It marked a crossroads in a career that had started when he was searching for golf balls at the Brynhill club, Barry, as an eleven-year-old.

Dodd, born in 1966, just a fortnight before that unforgettable English triumph in the football World Cup final, was fortunate to have one of the finest junior golf structures in the country on his doorstep. Under the guidance of junior leader John Collins, who managed a stable that included a string of Welsh title holders at various levels, Dodd always stood out as a great natural talent, if a little too relaxed for his own good times.

His first senior international appearances for Wales came as a teenager in 1985, after he had reached the semi-finals of the Welsh Amateur Championship at Ashburnham. But a few months later Dodd, along with fellow Welsh team members John Peters and Mike Macara, were dropped from the squad and disciplined following an incident at a training camp in La Manga, Spain.

All three were ruled out of the 1986 Home Internationals while Dodd and Macara were also barred from the Welsh Amateur Championship and the Welsh Open Strokeplay.

For Dodd, whose first appearance in the Home Internationals had been extremely encouraging, it was a significant setback. On his day he was the outstanding golfer in Wales, as his three victories in four years (1985, '86 and '88) in the Welsh Brewers Champion of Champions tournament clearly illustrated. However, the major titles continued to elude him until that glorious 1989 season when everything clicked into place.

His narrow victory in the Welsh Open Strokeplay at Conwy, one stroke ahead of Phillip Price, not only earned Dodd his first major national title, but also put him in the spotlight in front of watching Walker Cup selector Rodney James and captain Geoff Marks.

'It was a major confidence boost for me at the time because it got very tense down the stretch, and I suppose it was the catalyst for everything else which followed that season.'

What followed next was the Amateur Championship at Royal Birkdale, where Dodd would become the fourth Welsh winner in a golden decade, following in the footsteps of Duncan Evans (1980), Phil Parkin (1983) and Paul Mayo (1987).

After successfully negotiating a path to the final, only the unheralded England youth international Craig Casells stood between Dodd and the trophy. It was never in doubt, Dodd winning four of the first five holes and never being headed before closing out the match 5&3 in front of a gallery which included some 50 friends

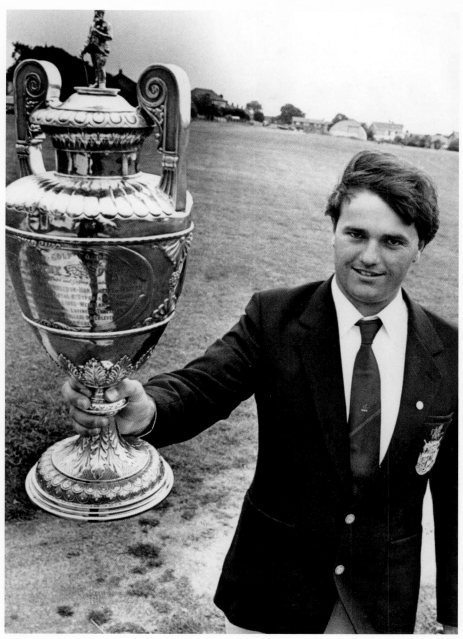

Dodd with the imposing Amateur Championship trophy after his 1989 victory at Royal Birkdale

*(Media Wales)*

from Brynhill, who had travelled up to Merseyside at the crack of dawn after being scrambled by John Collins.

'To have so many people on the course supporting me was a huge boost and I was so glad they were able to join in the celebrations after coming all that way.'

With invitations to the Open Championship and the US Masters in the bag, Dodd could have been forgiven for getting a little carried away himself, but he declined the offer of a few glasses of champagne, instead celebrating with a diet lemonade in the press tent.

Craig Defoy, Wales's national coach at the time, probably summed up Dodd perfectly after watching his Birkdale success:

'Stephen was without doubt the most natural player I had ever worked with. Quite frankly I don't think he realised himself just how good he was.'

From there, Dodd returned home to help Wales finish fifth in the European Team Championships at Royal Porthcawl, after which he was, as expected, named in the Walker Cup team to travel to Atlanta. But before that, he had time to win the Welsh Amateur Championship at Tenby, defeating defending champion Keith Jones 2&1 in the final and becoming the first player since Jimmy Buckley in 1968 to capture both the strokeplay and matchplay titles in the same season.

Then came The Open, where Dodd had the honour of being paired with the legendary Arnold Palmer during the first two rounds. He missed the cut after cards of 79 and 75, but will never forget the experience.

'To play in The Open as a pro is fantastic but to be there as an amateur was incredible. The R&A always tend to give the Amateur Champion a decent draw, but to be out alongside Arnold Palmer was special.'

And so to Peachtree, where Dodd contributed one win and two halves in his four outings as GB&I gained an historic 12½-11½ win over a USA team including a certain Phil Mickelson.

There was one more accolade to follow for Dodd, and perhaps the one that he expected least of all as he was named Western Mail Welsh Sports Personality of the Year for 1989, the fourth golfer to be honoured following Dai Rees (1957), Duncan Evans (1980) and Ian Woosnam (1987).

'To be honest it was a bit of a shock, but a pleasant one. Some great names have won the award and to join them was a real honour. It was the icing on the cake of a great year for me.'

While his fellow Walker Cup teammate Neil Roderick, along with Keith Jones and Phillip Price, all departed for the professional ranks that autumn, Dodd, at the age of 23, had every reason to hang around.

'A lot of people were maybe expecting me to turn pro after the season I'd had, but playing in the US Masters was just too good an opportunity to miss out on.'

In preparation Dodd accepted an invitation to play in the Australian Masters at the start of the year and then, along with a group of Brynhill members, he headed to South Carolina for some practice before moving on to Augusta along with his parents Brian and Meryl, younger brother Andrew, coach Peter Johnson and John Perry, who regularly caddied for him.

Dodd, in the company of Major winners Curtis Strange and Sandy Lyle, acquitted himself well at Augusta but rounds of 77 and 78 saw him miss the cut as Nick Faldo went on to claim the coveted green jacket.

'It's everything that you expect it to be and a lot more. The whole Masters week is incredible and there's no way I would have missed it.'

Back home, Dodd was expected to defend his Amateur Championship title at Muirfield. However, in a surprise move, he announced in May that he was turning professional with immediate effect and linked up with the St Mary's club at Pencoed, near Bridgend.

Expectations were inevitably high given his amateur record, but things didn't work out quite as planned.

'It was never going to be easy, and those who thought that my amateur record would mean I was going to get success overnight as a pro were way off the mark. I had to change my game considerably and altered my swing a lot to cope with the demands of the professional game. There was a hell of a lot that I didn't know, and it takes time to adapt.'

There were some successes. In 1991 Dodd won the West Region PGA Championship at St Mary's and in 1995 he claimed the Welsh PGA title at Northop Country Park. But on the Tour it was a tough existence. From 1991 to 1994, Dodd laboured with limited success on the second tier Challenge Tour, winning once, in Austria in 1992. He gained a full card for 1995 through the qualifying school, lost it, but regained it via the same route for 1996.

The yo-yo effect continued with two more seasons on the Challenge Tour in 1996 and 1997, and another in 2000 after four more failed attempts to make an impact among the elite.

The breakthrough came in 2001 when Dodd finished 97th on the Order of Merit, thus retaining his full card for the first time without having to return to the qualifying school. For the next three years there was a steady, if unspectacular, improvement as Dodd began to establish himself as a mid-ranking Tour pro. Then came his big moment in China, followed by the Irish Open success after a thrilling play-off with Ryder Cup man David Howell.

His 2005 earnings broke through the one million Euro barrier, he was 17th on the Order of Merit, and there was a call up to Colin Montgomerie's GB&I team which defeated Seve Ballesteros's continentals to win the Seve Trophy at The Wynyard in County Durham.

Rounding things off was the World Cup win on the Algarve, Dodd and Bradley Dredge emulating the achievements of Ian Woosnam and David Llewellyn in Hawaii eighteen years earlier and splitting the £900,000 prize money.

Dodd's by now legendary laid-back approach came to the fore when Wales, leading after the third round, had to sit in the clubhouse and watch the torrential rain which eventually forced the cancellation of the final round.

'We would have liked to have gone out on a nice sunny final day and finished things off in style. We had played some great golf for three days and we were ready to do the same again before the weather intervened. But we were leading and so we deserved to win. It was a huge result for Welsh golf given the standard of opposition.'

Dodd's European Open success at the K Club in 2006, less than a week away from his 40th birthday, catapulted him to 16th on the Ryder Cup points list and in with a great chance of making a return to the Irish course in the European Team. However, despite finishing 29th on the Order of Merit with almost 800,000 euros, his form tailed off towards the crucial end-of-season run-in.

The 2007 season was a disappointment as Dodd slipped to 122nd on the Order of Merit, and 2008 was even worse as increasing injury worries saw him plummet to 245th and his world ranking slumped as low as 794.

As important as his recovery from knee problems, from a hairline fracture in a wisdom tooth and a mystery virus contracted in Asia, was Dodd completely revisiting his golf swing with his long-time coach, Terry Hanson, professional at the Cardiff golf club.

'What I saw on camera left me pretty much horrified,' reflected Dodd. 'I felt I needed to take time off from the European Tour and try and get things back to where they were when I won three events and the World Cup with Bradley.

'I really don't know how many things I changed in my swing, but it was a lot. Luckily I had the European Tour exemption to 2011 to fall back on. It would have been a complete nightmare trying to make radical changes to your game while trying to earn enough money to keep your card. That made the decision to take time out a whole lot easier.'

And having shown previously that he can live with the best, Dodd set about getting back there with a vastly improved 2009 season which saw him re-established in 62nd place on the Order of Merit and a position alongside Jamie Donaldson in Wales's World Cup of Golf team.

That ice-cool temperament which many have mistaken for a lack of ambition, will no doubt continue to serve him well. There has never been any whooping and hollering from Dodd, and don't expect that to change.

Or as Ian Woosnam so eloquently put it: 'Stephen can do well in the big events because he's so cool under pressure. I'd love to put a monitor on him because I don't think he has a heartbeat!'

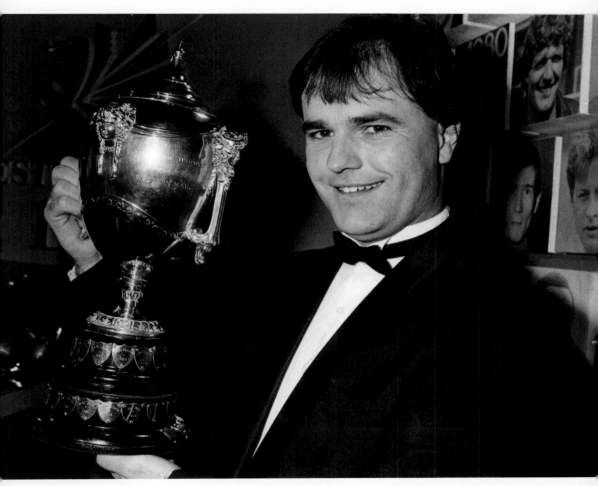

Stephen Dodd pictured with the 1989 Western Mail/BBC Welsh Sports Personality of the Year award

Nigel Edwards

# Chapter Sixteen
# Nigel Edwards

IN a sport, and an age, where almost every talented player aspires to turn professional at the first available opportunity, Nigel Edwards stands out from the crowd.

No other Welshman can boast a Walker Cup record to match that of the 41-year-old Whitchurch golfer, the four Great Britain and Ireland tour bags standing side by side in his office at the Golf Union of Wales headquarters a testament to the remarkable achievements of this 'career' amateur.

But no one should ever be fooled into thinking that Edwards's decision to stay out of the professional game shows any lack of ambition. In fact, quite the opposite is true of a man who has shown more determination than most, and who has become one of the world's top amateurs. Not bad for someone who was once told he was not good enough to make the Welsh Boys' team.

First introduced to the game by a friend, Simon English, whose parents were members at Bargoed Golf Club, Edwards was brought up on the Troedyrhiw estate in Ystrad Mynach.

'There were a group of us, all mates, who used to go and whack a ball,' he recalled. 'When I was eleven, my father brought home a broken, cut-down nine iron and I started hitting balls in a field nearby. I was hooked.'

The young Edwards joined Bryn Meadows in the winter of 1980 and spent his formative years there before joining Whitchurch in 1985. He has been a member of the club ever since and was honoured in 2002 with life membership.

The road that would ultimately lead to those four Walker Cup appearances started in far more humble surroundings, the Gwent Golf Union junior summer medals being the breeding ground for Edwards.

'I remember the first one I played in at Pontnewydd, and I was given a handicap of 33. I shot a net 27 for nine holes after starting with a double bogey. I won the competition, my handicap was slashed and I was given three golf balls. At the time it felt like winning the Open Championship.'

Edwards, a pupil at Lewis School, Pengam, where he was followed a few years later by Bradley Dredge, continued to progress through the junior scene in Gwent. In 1984 he was runner-up in the Welsh Boys' strokeplay championship and the following year reached the semi-finals of the South Wales Boys' matchplay at Neath. He was also part of the Gwent side who won the Severnside tournament at Ross-on-Wye in 1985 and the Lewis side who reached the grand finals of the Golf Foundation Schools' team championships at Sunningdale in 1985 and Foxhills in 1986, where he was thrilled to meet the legendary Sir Henry Cotton, who passed away shortly after.

'I remember the feeling of disappointment a couple of times when I thought I had done enough to get in the Welsh Boys' team only to hear the names being called out and mine not being among them. I think my determination was fuelled by those setbacks and a few people find it hard to believe now that I never played for Wales as a junior.'

After completing his A-level studies, Edwards moved straight into the world of work, securing a job within the Highways Department at Mid Glamorgan County Council.

'I was playing county golf for Glamorgan but with work, and doing a civil engineering course in college, it was difficult to devote too much time to it.'

Despite juggling a full-time job and part-time studies, Edwards started to make some ripples on the Welsh circuit, reaching the quarter-finals of the 1993 Welsh Amateur Championship before losing to Dredge, who would go on to earn a Walker Cup place later that year.

'After sitting my college exams in 1993, I had some decent results but 1994 turned out to be a disappointment and I think I was trying a bit too hard to make an impression. The start of 1995 was also pretty quiet but then I got to the British Amateur at Hoylake and played well to qualify comfortably for the matchplay. I beat Padraig Harrington, which gave me a lot of confidence, but then lost to the New Zealander, Marcus Wheelhouse.'

Having been bypassed by the Welsh selectors up to that point, Edwards's performances finally made them sit up and take notice and his first cap came in the Home Internationals at Royal Portrush that autumn.

'Getting my blazer and badge after so long was great, but the thing I remember most was just the buzz of being able to play on such a fantastic golf course with so many good players. I was paired with my former Gwent colleague Andrew Harrhy in the opening foursomes against England and I got a rude awakening as we went six down after seven against Matthew Blackey and David Lynn before eventually losing 3&2. But then I beat Gary Clark at the 17th in the singles and helped us defeat England for the first time in 25 years.'

Edwards would become a permanent fixture in the Wales team thereafter, his run in the Home Internationals only interrupted in 2003 when he withdrew to be with wife Jane, who was due to give birth to their first child, Tomos.

Playing for Wales was an ambition achieved, but Edwards admits that he still found it difficult to be playing head-to-head with the likes of Harrington, who would, of course, go on to become a Ryder Cup regular and the Open Champion in 2007 and 2008, the year in which he also won the USPGA title.

'Back in 1995 I still felt that the Harringtons and Dredges of the world were just so far away from me. My determination and attitude were never a problem but I didn't feel like my game was in the same league as theirs.'

Significantly, Harrington, Dredge and many others were 'professional' amateurs, and able to concentrate almost exclusively on golf. At the same time, Edwards was relying on the goodwill of his employers (who granted him paid leave when he represented Wales) and some complex balancing acts with his holiday entitlement. It was in 1999 that Edwards changed his career and became a full time official of the Welsh Golfing Union, being appointed to the role of golf co-ordinator. By then he had already been in the Walker Cup squad, but missed out on selection for the 1999 matches.

Edwards, left, caddying for his former Wales amateur team-mate Bradley Dredge during a Europro Tour event at The Vale in 2004

*(Media Wales)*

'I suppose most people thought that working for the Welsh Golfing Union would allow me to play golf whenever I wanted, but it wasn't quite as straightforward as that. When I first started, I was involved in the running of several of the Welsh championship events and that meant I couldn't play.'

As his role has evolved – he is now Director of Player Development and Coaching at the Golf Union of Wales – so he has managed his time efficiently enough to be able to play in enough of the major tournaments to keep him at the very top of the sport.

'The Union have been very good to me and very supportive, and Celtic Manor have helped me enormously with the use of the facilities. But the bottom line is that I have a job to do and I'm sure if I wasn't doing that job to the required standard my employers would have something to say.'

The 2000 and 2001 seasons underlined Edwards's growing stature in the amateur game and a remarkable course record 65 in the Lytham Trophy at Royal Lytham was one of the highlights which helped secure him a Walker Cup debut at Ocean Forest, Sea Island, Georgia.

Part of arguably the most talented GB&I team ever to leave these shores – Nick Dougherty, Graeme McDowell and Marc Warren have all gone on to become winners on the European Tour while Luke Donald has won in Europe and America and played in two Ryder Cups – Edwards played in only one of the four series of matches, losing 5&4 to Nick Cassini in the Saturday singles.

'I had been to Ocean Forest at the start of 2001 to play in the Jones Cup and I was determined to get back there for the Walker Cup. It was definitely a step up from anything I had done before and I was taken out of my comfort zone. I only played once and didn't play that well, but the bottom line is that it's a team event and I was part of a team that won 15-9.

'The captain Peter McEvoy sent me a letter when we got home and told me he knew I was disappointed to play only once out of the four series of matches but I would be a key player for GB&I in the future. That was something he didn't have to do and it underlined what a great captain he was.'

Consistency for the next two seasons ensured that Edwards would get the chance to set the record straight in the 2003 matches at Ganton, something he achieved in a style few who were there will ever forget.

Edwards and fellow Welshman Stuart Manley became the backbone of Garth McGimpsey's team, with one win and one half in their foursomes outings. In the opening days singles, Edwards overcame the veteran American George Zahringer 3&2 and by the time he and Manley teed off in the two anchor singles on the final afternoon, it was clear that they would have a key role in the outcome.

'I suppose if ever a course suited me then it was Ganton that week. The team didn't have the "stars" of 2001 and we went in as underdogs but produced some fantastic golf under pressure.'

Pressure was certainly the by-word on the final afternoon as, with the matches balanced on a knife edge, Edwards and Manley were out at the back of the field. Edwards and his opponent Lee Williams were involved in a classic, the Welshman showing steely determination, coolness and raw emotion in equal quantities as he chipped in from off the 14th green and then rolled in a tramliner of a putt from the edge of the 17th.

His half point, and Manley's 3&1 win over Trip Kuehne at the bottom of the order, ensured GB&I gained a dramatic 12½-11½ overall victory to retain the Cup. For Edwards it was probably the weekend when his own golf game rose to new levels in front of an 8,000 crowd and a few million more on live television.

Two years down the line in Chicago, Edwards, now one of the mainstays of the team, was involved in more drama, on the course and off it.

'Jane was pregnant with Tomos and at the USGA dinner the night before the matches started, she fainted. Then my mother collapsed with dehydration during the opening ceremony and was taken to hospital.'

Thankfully both recovered quickly, but by the final afternoon their blood pressure might have needed monitoring again as Edwards was embroiled in another make-or-break singles at the bottom of the order against Jeff Overton, whom he had lost 5&4 to the previous day.

This time Edwards just failed to match the heroics of Ganton, a miraculous par at the 17th by Overton and a putt that stayed agonisingly above ground on the last settling the issue as the Americans took the honours 12½-11½.

The disappointment of Chicago was quickly shaken off as Edwards started 2006 with one of the individual highlights of his career, a victory in the South African Amateur Championship. That earned him a place in the South African Open, where he played the first two rounds in the company of Retief Goosen and Lee Westwood. It gave Edwards, who has also played in the Wales Open on the European Tour, a taste of the professional game. Inevitably it also drew the question as to whether Edwards ever regretted not trying his luck in the paid ranks.

'I've never been good enough at a time when it would have been possible to turn pro,' is his honest assessment. 'If I'd been playing at such a high level a few years earlier then maybe it would have been different.'

Victory in the Sherry Cup in Sotogrande and fourth place with Wales in the World Team Championships for the Eisenhower Trophy added up to an impressive year, and a string of consistent results at the start of 2007 cemented his appearance in the GB&I team for a fourth Walker Cup at Royal County Down.

Once again, after a remarkable final day fightback by GB&I, Edwards found himself in the spotlight, his singles match with Jonathan Moore thrilling the most vociferous and enthusiastic galleries the event has ever seen. It was Moore who prevailed after a sensational second shot to the par-five 18th which set up a match-winning eagle. On any other day Edwards's own birdie 4 would have been good enough for at least a half.

'I'm not really one for looking at leaderboards, but it was pretty obvious that it was a pivotal match given the galleries and all the attention. I played the 16th, 17th and 18th well all week and if you lose to an eagle you can't really get down on yourself.'

Edwards's hopes of matching the five successive Walker appearances of the great Englishman McEvoy were ended with his non-selection in the final squad for the 2009 matches at Merion, Pennsylvania. But, typically, Edwards took the news with a deal of philosophy and good grace.

'My omission from the squad was disappointing but you've got to dust yourself down and get back up again. You get over it, it isn't life or death.

*(Media Wales)*

Edwards in action during the 2003 Welsh Amateur championship at Southerndown

As one door closes another opens, and for Edwards that was in December 2009 when a phone call from the R&A's Chairman of Selectors – fellow Welshman Tony Disley – brought an early Christmas present for Edwards, the Walker Cup captaincy. Edwards was offered, and accepted, the role for the 2010 St Andrews Trophy matches against continental Europe and the 2011 Walker Cup at Royal Aberdeen.

So, having been such an influential figure in a playing capacity, Edwards will now be masterminding GB&I's bid to wrest the cup back from the Americans.

'I was aware that my name had been mentioned in connection with the job but it still came as a surprise, and a huge honour, to get that call from the R&A.

Nigel Edwards in action at the Cardiff Feathers tournament at Cardiff Golf Club

'I have played under some fantastic captains both for Wales and GB&I and I'd like to think that some of the things I've learned from them, as well as my own philosophies on the game, will stand me in good stead.'

Edwards will become only the third Welshman to fill the role, after Tony Duncan and Clive Brown. So does this mean we have seen the last of Nigel Edwards as a player?

'I certainly think my playing commitments will be fewer than they have been. With a young family and a full-time job it becomes increasingly difficult year after year to play in all tournaments necessary to compete at the highest level. It's not so much the tournaments but more the time needed to practise. You can't survive at the top level of amateur golf on ten minutes a day at the driving range.

'I'm in a position now where I can pick and choose when I want to play so we'll wait and see.'

If he never plays international golf again – and he surely will – Edwards has proved himself to be among the greats of the amateur game. Four successive Walker Cups equates to a decade of consistency at the pinnacle of his sport.

'If someone had told me a few years ago that I'd be looking back at four Walker Cup matches, I probably wouldn't have believed them. It's something I'm very proud of, and not bad for someone who people thought wasn't good enough to play for Wales.'

Bradley Dredge

## Chapter Seventeen
# Bradley Dredge

IN 2005 Bradley Dredge banked £1.1m in prize money and held the status of a World Cup winner.

Such fame and fortune could easily have knocked a less level-headed individual out of kilter. But being caught up in the events of Boxing Day 2004 in South East Asia gave Dredge a sense of perspective that no amount of success is likely to change.

Dredge and his wife Germaine headed off to Thailand, a favourite holiday destination of theirs, for Christmas and the New Year. And when they left Wales, the word 'Tsunami' wasn't even in the dictionary, but the tragic deaths of more than 220,000 people across the islands of Indonesia, Thailand, Malaysia and Sri Lanka changed that forever.

The Dredges left Phuket just three days before the Tsunami waves struck the tourist hotspot with catastrophic loss of life. But that was just the first near-miss as they headed 120km south to Pangkor Island, off the Malaysian coast.

'We found out later Pangkor was on a direct line to the earthquake epicentre in Sumatra and we were on a beach-front location,' he recalled. 'Luckily for us it escaped the worst and the island was only hit by a few of the smaller waves.

'When we found out the following day the extent of the devastation and how many people had lost their lives, we just had to pack up and return home.'

'Level headed' is a term often associated with Dredge, who seems the most likely prospect of Wales having a playing interest in the 2010 Ryder Cup on what is, for him, the familiar territory of the Celtic Manor Resort. And earning Ryder Cup honours would be the pinnacle of a career that has seen Dredge steadily progress from one of Britain's finest amateurs to a genuine contender for the major honours in the European game.

It's all a far cry from the days when he helped out in his mother's tea rooms in Blackwood before heading to Bryn Meadows golf club where he spent hour after hour on the practice ground. Born in Blackwood in July 1973, Dredge was educated at the Lewis School, Pengam, and, like so many who go on to reach the highest levels of their sport, was something of an all-rounder.

As well as golf, Dredge was a useful fast bowler for the Rhymney Valley schools, a scrum-half at rugby, and demonstrated no little potential as a 400m athlete. He was also one of the best young snooker players around and if things had turned out differently he could well have continued Gwent's rich tradition of green baize masters which included six-times World champion Ray Reardon, Doug Mountjoy, Darren Morgan and, most recently, another former World title holder Mark Williams.

'I was having a poor spell at snooker and so I decided to stick with golf and the rest is history.'

His father Roger, himself a useful six-handicapper, taught him the rudiments of the game and then he came under the wing of Bryn Meadows professional Bruce Hunter and the club's owner, the late Brian Mayo, who became Dredge's mentor and number one supporter. And once he had established himself as one of the brightest prospects in the Welsh game, he was coached by Newport professional Paul Mayo, himself a former amateur star of distinction and European Tour professional.

The Welsh Boys' title in 1991 was his first national championship win and Great Britain and Ireland junior honours followed in the same season as he was a member of the victorious Jacques Leglise Trophy team against the Continent of Europe.

The transition from junior to senior golf can be difficult for some, but Dredge seemed to make it seamlessly.

In 1992 he was simply outstanding, although his season didn't exactly start with a flourish as he struggled round Southerndown in 84 in the opening round of the Duncan Putter over the Easter weekend. But he won the Carmarthenshire Open Order of Merit event the very next weekend then headed north to finish runner-up to Andrew Barnett in the Welsh Open Strokeplay at Royal St David's, and lifted the Gold Cross title at the same venue.

The teenager finished second in both the European Individual Amateur Championship in Rome and the Irish Youths' Open at Clandeboye and led the individual qualifiers in the European Youths' Team Championships in Helsinki, before taking four points out of five in the matchplay rounds.

In the Amateur Championship at Carnoustie, Dredge reached the final before losing to the unheralded Scot Stephen Dundas, a defeat that cost him invitations to both the US Masters and the Open Championship.

'It was a great season for me but losing the final at Carnoustie was a big disappointment. The difference between winning and losing that one match is a world apart. Win and you go to the Masters and the Open, lose and you just get a pat on the back.'

Still, there was some consolation in that Dredge's outstanding form over the whole summer caught the attention of the GB&I selectors who named him in the four-man Eisenhower Trophy team to contest the World Championships in Vancouver, Canada, the first Welsh player to be afforded the honour.

At that stage Dredge appeared to be a certainty for a Walker Cup spot in the GB&I team to take on the United States at Interlachen, Minneapolis, the following

August. However, his early-season form in 1993 was less impressive than it had been twelve months earlier, and it was not until the European Team Championships in the Czech Republic that Dredge cemented his place. There he was part of the six-man Welsh team, under the captaincy of John Jermine, who created history by bringing the title back to the Principality.

'In amateur terms Bradley was a world-class player and was an integral part of the best Welsh team ever to take part in a European event,' recalled Jermine. 'He was always focused, always willing to listen to advice, and always in control of his own game.'

When Dredge was named in the GB&I side, with the pressure lifted from his shoulders, he won the Tucker Trophy and, a fortnight later, took the Welsh Amateur Championship at Southerndown, beating Matthew Ellis in the final.

Dredge was widely expected to turn professional after the Walker Cup, but in the wake of GB&I's crushing 19-5 defeat – one of the heaviest in the history of the series – he announced that he would be staying in the amateur ranks. And there was also the incentive of setting the Walker Cup record straight in 1995, and on Welsh soil at Royal Porthcawl, with a Welshman, Clive Brown, at the helm.

'The fact the Walker Cup was in Wales was a big factor because I wanted to have another chance. You never know how things are going to turn out in golf and unfortunately for me it didn't work out as I'd hoped.'

Although he retained his GB&I place for the St Andrews Trophy matches against the Continent of Europe at Chantilly in 1994, Dredge never made the Walker Cup team the following autumn and missed out on the opportunity of taking on an American side which included

Dredge playing for Wales in the Home Internationals

*(Media Wales)*

123

Tiger Woods. And while Brown's team was celebrating a momentous win at Porthcawl, Dredge was finalising his plans to join the paid ranks.

He failed to gain a European Tour card at the qualifying school in 1995 and spent 1996 playing on the domestic circuit before embarking on a first full season on the Challenge Tour in 1997.

And what a first season it was. Dredge had his wife caddying for him as he secured his maiden Tour title in the Klassis Turkish Open. With the top fifteen on the Order of Merit gaining full Tour cards for 1998, Dredge went into the final event of the season in sixteenth position. And in the Estoril Grand Final, an event reduced to 54 holes due to the weather, the nails were bitten down to the quick as Dredge finished tied eighth and moved up one place to claim the last golden ticket.

'After the third round I checked the standings and knew that if I finished eighth it would be good enough to move me into fifteenth spot. I don't think I've ever been so glad to see torrential rain.'

His first experience of life with the big guns in 1998 proved to be a steep learning curve, and after just one top-20 finish in South Africa, Dredge finished 157th on the money list and was back on the Challenge Tour for 1999.

Four top-ten finishes, including a victory in the Is Molas Challenge in Sardinia, saw Dredge finish eighth on the Order of Merit and secure a return to the main Tour for 2000. This time he was there for the long haul. And his three top-tens enabled him to consolidate his status with 107th place on the Order of Merit, an improvement which continued in 2001 with two more top-tens on his way to 72nd spot.

In 2002 Dredge finished eighteenth on the money list with just under one million Euros, enjoying a remarkable ten top-tens.

Now it was just a matter of getting that all-important first victory, and it arrived in spectacular fashion in 2003 at Santo da Serra, venue for the Madeira Island Open. Dredge left the whole field trailing in his wake in the third round with the lowest score of his career, a 12-under-par 60, and could afford to cruise around on Sunday with a 71 and still win by eight shots.

'I'd waited a long time to get a win, and I always envisaged having to hole a nerve-wracking putt for it. As it turned out, I had eight putts from a few feet which is pretty unusual, but a lot easier on the nerves. You get a bit tired of people asking when you are going to win, especially as I'd had a lot of top-tens over the previous couple of years.'

It was a case of 'after the Lord Mayor's show' in 2004 as Dredge finished 60th on the money list, but then came that memorable 2005 with a career high sixteenth, another eight top-ten finishes, and the honour of holing the winning putt for Colin Montgomerie's GB&I team in their Seve Trophy victory against the continental Europeans at The Wynyard.

Dredge home at Bryn Meadows

*(Media Wales)*

The World Cup victory with Stephen Dodd in the Algarve, after the final day's play was washed out, proved to be the icing on a very large cake.

'To follow in the footsteps of Woosie and David Llewellyn in 1987 was a huge honour for me and Stephen. It's the biggest event I can compete in exclusively for Wales so it's extra special. It was a bit frustrating with the rain on the final day and we'd have liked to have won it over the full distance, but we were happy to take it.'

Great things were expected of Dredge in 2006, and many felt he would play his way into Ian Woosnam's Ryder Cup side for the matches at the K Club in the autumn.

Again there were plenty of high finishes, but Dredge didn't quite do enough to make the team, and ironically, the biggest win of his career came just after Woosnam's line-up had been finalised.

Dredge went to Crans Sur Sierre in the Swiss Alps and destroyed a top quality field to win the Omega European Masters – again by eight shots. He then went to Scotland and set a course record 64 for the newly lengthened Old Course at St Andrews on his way to runner-up spot in the Dunhill Links Championship.

He ended the year 22nd on the Order of Merit and with a call up to the combined Europe/America team to play the Rest of the World in the Goodwill Trophy in China. In 2007 Dredge confirmed his place among Europe's elite by finishing 23rd on the Order of Merit, just missing out on a third Tour title when edged out in a play-off at the Irish Open by Padraig Harrington, who would, of course, go on to become Open Champion a short while later at Carnoustie.

After all those years of heartbreak, from missing out on a place in the US Masters through to the Amateur Championship, Dredge finally made it to Augusta for his debut after breaking into the world's top 50. A disastrous final round apart, it proved to be a hugely encouraging debut at that.

He was also runner-up in the Wales Open at Celtic Manor and retained his place in Nick Faldo's GB&I Seve Trophy team which retained the silverware at The Heritage in Ireland. Faldo, the vanquished European Ryder Cup skipper for the 2008 matches at Valhalla, Kentucky, was suitably impressed as Dredge went through the weekend unbeaten with four-and-a-half points from a possible five. The six-time Major winner would not have been disappointed had Dredge been among his charges at Valhalla, but it was not to be.

Despite three top-ten finishes in the 2008 season, Dredge ended up 74th on the money list, his lowest placing since 2000. 2009, however, saw a climb to 57th, but it remains to be seen whether 2010 will be the year that Dredge achieves his Ryder Cup ambitions?

'The Ryder Cup is the ultimate team event in golf and every player's dream to compete in. I'm no different. My goal is to accumulate enough points to qualify and I think it's a realistic goal for me. I believe it's the right time in my career to step up and challenge for a place. I want to be at Celtic Manor to play rather than to watch. It would be phenomenal for a Welshman to make the team, and it's a big incentive for the likes of Stephen Dodd, Jamie Donaldson, Phil Price and myself.'

Only time will tell, but after Bert Hodson, Dai Rees, Dave Thomas, Brian Huggett, Ian Woosnam and Phil Price, the next chapter in Wales's Ryder Cup history could well be in the hands of Bradley Dredge.

A relaxed Bradley Dredge playing in a Wales Open pro-am at Celtic Manor

Becky Morgan

# Chapter Eighteen

# Becky Morgan

WHEN Becky Morgan arrived in Greensboro, North Carolina, in 1994, she never envisaged that well over a decade later she would still be Stateside flying a lone flag for Welsh women's golf on the LPGA Tour.

Now based in the Florida sunshine along with, as she puts it, 'Every other golf pro in the world,' Morgan has adapted to life and golf in the USA far better than many predicted that a shy youngster from Abergavenny would.

In 2008 the path from the amateur game at junior level in Great Britain and Ireland to the cut-throat world of US collegiate golf has become well worn, but in 1994 Morgan was taking a step largely into the unknown. And at that stage, a career in professional golf was not at the top of Morgan's agenda, but the lack of opportunities in Britain to pursue a degree while continuing to play as an amateur at the highest level forced her to cast the net further afield.

'To be honest, at the time you only had St Andrews and Stirling Universities as realistic options if you wanted to combine golf and studying in Britain, and I just felt they weren't for me,' said Morgan, whose Welsh accent has survived the intervening decade and more with only a minor hint of an American drawl. 'I knew a few acquaintances who had been through the US College system and so I started looking into the possibilities of a scholarship. There were a few offers but eventually I settled on the University of North Carolina and it proved to be a great choice.'

Born in Abergavenny in 1974 along with twin sister Rachel, Morgan's golf career started at the age of twelve when her grandfather introduced her to the game at the picturesque Monmouth golf club. Up to that point, Morgan had played football, badminton, tennis and lacrosse as she demonstrated her all-round sporting ability. Whilst her sister's enthusiasm for the game of golf dwindled, Becky Morgan was hooked, and was soon attracting attention outside the confines of Monmouth.

A regular in the Welsh Girls' team, Morgan won the Welsh Schools' title in 1991 and defended it successfully the following year. However, it was that decision to cross the Atlantic which would enable Morgan to take a quantum leap in her golf career.

'I know my parents worried because I was quite a shy girl, but North Carolina is a friendly place and I think I settled down more quickly than anyone, including myself, thought I would.'

Settle down she did, Morgan embarking on a highly successful collegiate career that would earn her ten NCAA Division I titles, including three successive Big South Conference Championships from 1995-1997.

Morgan shelters from the elements during the Welsh
Ladies' Championship of Europe at Machynys in 2006

*(Media Wales)*

'As far as my golf game was concerned, America was a fantastic learning experience. The collegiate circuit is so competitive and you have to be on your game all the time. There are just so many good players and everyone is hungry for success.'

In 1997, the year she graduated, majoring in Geography, Morgan finished tenth in the season-ending NCAA Championships, and was named as a second-team All American.

The improvement in her golf game while in North Carolina was clearly evident on her trips back home, most notably for the British Women's Open Championship, one of the flagship events in the amateur game. Thus in 1996, over the Royal Liverpool links at Hoylake, Morgan reached the final only to lose out 5&3 against the talented American prodigy Kelli Kuehne. Twelve months later at Cruden Bay in the north of Scotland she was a semi-finalist. And those performances went a long way to earning Morgan a Great Britain and Ireland call up for the Vagliano Trophy matches against Continental Europe.

Now established as one of the leading lights not just in Wales, but in Great Britain, Morgan's stock was still rising when she returned to Wales following her graduation to continue her amateur career.

1998 was a standout year as she reached the final of the Welsh championship, was runner-up in the British Women's Strokeplay and played for GB&I in the narrow 10-8 Curtis Cup defeat against the Americans in Minneapolis. But having retained her place in the team beaten by the same score at Ganton in 2000, Morgan then found herself at the crossroads of her career, and facing a dilemma as to which route she would follow.

'I know most players who come through the amateur ranks and reach a high level just naturally aspire to turn pro, but I wasn't totally sure that it was the right thing for me to do,' reflected Morgan.

Ultimately Morgan did decide to join the paid ranks, but maximised her chances of success by entering the Tour qualifying schools on both sides of the Atlantic in the autumn of 2000.

Consistency had been her hallmark as an amateur, and that same trait stood her in good stead in the heat of the battle for Tour cards. She finished tied sixth to earn her playing rights on the European Tour and finished tied fourteenth at the final LPGA Tour School to secure partial playing privileges in the USA.

'You have to take your chances and I was lucky enough to take a little bit of the pressure off myself by earning opportunities to play on both tours. I had a top-ten finish (17th) in one of my early tournaments of 2001 in America (The Longs Drugs Challenge) and that gave me the opportunity to play in a lot more. The fact that I started so well in America probably shaped my whole career. If I hadn't achieved any results early on, I would more than likely have returned home to play more on the European Tour.'

Morgan's first pro season in the States saw her play 16 events, and she was beaten to the Rookie of the Year award only by South Korea's Hee Won Han. She also featured in eight European Tour events, making the cut in every one, posting four top-ten finishes and just missing out on a maiden win in the French Open when Norway's Suzann Pettersen denied her in a play-off.

After such a successful rookie year, 2002 was always going to be difficult for Morgan as she continued her professional apprenticeship.Eighteen LPGA tournaments yielded only one top-ten finish, but there were two more from just four starts in Europe. By 2003 Morgan was firmly established as a Tour regular and a career-best tied second at the ShopRite LPGA Classic was one of seven top-tens. Given her form Stateside, Morgan played just six events in Europe in 2003, but many felt that her form merited a wild card for Europe's Solheim Cup team.

She was leading the LPGA Tour stats in driving accuracy and on that side of the Atlantic most pundits had her pencilled in for a wild card berth. It was also felt that her amateur matchplay experience, both as an individual and as part of the Curtis Cup teams, was also in her favour. But European captain Catrin Nilsmark opted for Scotland's Janice Moodie instead, although Morgan would not allow herself to get bitter at missing out, even when she could have been forgiven for doing so.

'There was a lot of talk about me getting a wild card, but I knew from my amateur days that you can never take selection for granted. The captain picks who she thinks will do a job for the team and you have to respect those decisions.

'Yes I would love to have played and yes, I was disappointed, but you can't allow yourself to dwell on things. The next tournament comes along and you start looking forward again.'

Whether that is as close as Morgan gets to Solheim Cup selection remains to be seen, but since 2003 she has only sporadically hit the same heights. She does, however, remain a consistent money winner on Tour and 2009 was Morgan's ninth successive season inside the top-100 on the LPGA rankings.

A major factor behind that consistency is her placid temperament. Nothing much seems to faze Morgan and, unlike many of her contemporaries, she rarely loses control of her emotions on the golf course.

'I suppose that's just the way I am and I like to stay in control. Although I do remember launching a five-iron over the fence in anger once when things were not going well on the driving range. It was only the once, though.'

The introduction of the Women's World Cup of Golf has given Morgan, along with rising Welsh star Becky Brewerton, the opportunity to fly the Dragon on the biggest stage – and they have not disappointed, finishing sixth in 2005, third in 2006 and eighth in 2007. Similarly, the introduction of the Welsh Ladies' Championship of Europe, first at Royal Porthcawl and subsequently at Machynys Peninsula and Royal St David's, Harlech, has also afforded Morgan the opportunities to play in front of her home galleries, something she relishes.

In some ways the emergence of Brewerton put Morgan in the shade slightly, but she is more than happy to have another Welsh player making headlines.

'What Becky has achieved in becoming the first Welsh player to make the Solheim Cup team is great. There is no rivalry between us and we are good friends. If we are both doing well then it can only be good for women's golf in Wales. There are some very good young players coming through and hopefully we can be role models for them.

'Playing in the Championship of Europe over the last few years has been fantastic. After all, family and friends don't get too many opportunities to see me play when I'm in America so the support is always great and much appreciated.'

Brewerton may well decide that her long-term future lies in America too, but for the moment Morgan continues to plough a lone furrow for the Welsh professional game in the States.

'Home will always be Wales, and I get back every two to three months to see my family and my coach Renton Doig (the former St Pierre pro now based at Began Park). But I don't have any plans to move my base from the USA. The weather in Florida makes a huge difference and I still love the LPGA Tour. It remains the toughest but the best place to play golf.

'I believe I have the game to win tournaments and while my enthusiasm is still here I'll be giving it my best shot. I spend the winter months working hard

on my fitness in the gym and if I can stay injury-free then I'm confident I can make an impact at the highest level.

'Playing golf is what I do best and what I enjoy doing. It's a job most people would kill for, so I count myself lucky and try to make the most of it.'

Morgan has been something of a pioneer for the Welsh women's game and her diminutive 5ft 2in stature should fool no one. A determined competitor in the toughest arena in the women's game, she continues to prepare the ground for those who will follow.

*(Media Wales)*

Morgan plays out of a bunker at her home club, Monmouth, in 1997

Becky Brewerton

## Chapter Nineteen
# Becky Brewerton

BEING labelled 'The Next Big Thing' is never easy, and many a sportsman or woman has fallen by the wayside under the pressure of such a tag.

So there were plenty of sighs of relief and smiles all round when Becky Brewerton claimed her maiden victory on the Ladies' European Tour in the summer of 2007 and subsequently became Wales's first Solheim Cup player.

A precociously talented amateur with a record that few Welsh players before her could claim to have matched, Brewerton's arrival into the professional ranks was much anticipated. Especially so as she had gone close to claiming a European Tour title while still an amateur. A runners-up spot behind Germany's Elizabeth Esterl in the 2003 Tenerife Open, where she was playing on a sponsors' invitation, made the whole Tour sit up and take notice of this polite, but fiercely determined, young Welsh woman.

Amazingly she was second again on home soil in the Wales WPGA Championship of Europe at Royal Porthcawl, this time Australian Shani Waugh the only player to better her. So when she did officially join the paid ranks in November of that year, less than a month after her 21st birthday, the expectations and pressure on Brewerton were considerable. But she handled them like a seasoned veteran and, despite being without a victory until that memorable success in the English Open at Chart Hills, her Tour record was already looking pretty useful.

Brewerton has, from a very young age, been a winner. And winners are never fully satisfied unless they are winning.

'I'd been trying my hardest out there for so long, that to finally win was an unbelievable feeling,' she reflected.

What made it even more special for Brewerton was that her first professional win was watched by her father Steve and mother Paula, her two most trusted allies and loyal supporters. Steve had caddied for her throughout her amateur career and for the first few years on Tour before handing over the bag to the experienced Fred Collins.

'It was only the second event they had been to see me in during the season and with mum suffering from MS, she did so well to walk three rounds. It was so good to have them there, but I always thought they would be around when I got my first win.'

Born in St Asaph in 1982, Rebecca Dawn Brewerton first picked up a golf club at the age of twelve, and took to the sport like a duck to water. A product of the impressive junior set-up at Abergele Golf Club, Brewerton was already down to a 5 handicap by the age of 14, and it was in the summer of 1997 that the seeds of what was to become her career were sown.

Watching the Weetabix British Women's Open at Sunningdale on television, Brewerton was inspired. After seeing Australian Karrie Webb's victory, she was off to the driving range and eager to improve her game further. And that improvement came at a rate of knots, the Ysgol Glan Clwyd schoolgirl capturing the Welsh Girls' Championship title in 1997 and successfully defending it the following year – despite giving away two or three years experience to many of her rivals.

What followed was a stellar amateur career in senior golf with Welsh Championship wins at Conwy in 1999 and Royal St David's in 2001. Brewerton also captured the British Women's Strokeplay title in 1999 and was honoured with the prestigious Joyce Wethered award.

Those performances earned her a place in the Great Britain and Ireland Curtis Cup team to face the USA at Ganton in 2000. At 17, she was the youngest member of the team and one of the youngest in the history of the matches. Though the Americans won 10-8, despite a stirring comeback on the final day from the British side, Brewerton claimed one point out of three, a foursomes victory alongside Rebecca Hudson, and learned much from the experience.

'To be playing in a Curtis Cup at such a young age was amazing but the disappointment of losing was tough. It just made me more determined to get back into the team for 2002.'

That would not happen as Brewerton, despite retaining her GB&I place for the Vagliano Trophy in 2001, was controversially left out of the team to travel to Fox Chapel, Pennsylvania. Not only did the selectors decide that one of the most talented young players in the British Isles was not good enough to make the team of eight, but they named her only as a fourth reserve.

It was a blow that might have shattered the confidence of a lesser character, but Brewerton picked herself up and produced a series of performances that left a few of the selectors with extremely red faces.

Within a month of the team being announced, Brewerton had won the British Strokeplay for a second time and captured the European Individual Amateur title at Kristianstad, Sweden.

'I wouldn't say I was out to prove a point because I wanted to win every tournament I played, no matter what any selectors thought. I just went out to play my own game and ignore everything else. Of course I was bitterly disappointed. Looking back, I can never understand why I was in the team one year and then down to fourth reserve the next, and I never really got an answer as to why.

'I wasn't good enough to get into a team of eight, but a few months later I was picked for a team of three to play in the World Championships in Kuala Lumpur. Work that one out!'

Brewerton's amazing run of form in 2002 also saw her claim four-and-a-half points out of six for Wales in the Home Internationals at The Berkshire and she was named Daily Telegraph Golfer of the Year.

The 2003 season would be Brewerton's last as an amateur, and her performances the previous year had earned her a couple of invitations to play in European Tour events.

The first of those was in Tenerife in May where she held the lead at the halfway mark before eventually finishing second to Esterl. That result meant there was a huge focus on the youngster when she arrived at Porthcawl in August at the WPGA Championship of Europe.

And how close she came to securing a fairy-tale success! Her superb final round 70 in tough conditions looking as if it would be enough until Waugh sank an outrageous 70-foot putt at the last to deny her.

Had she been a pro, those two events would have earned Brewerton almost £55,000, and it was no surprise that she announced she would be leaving the amateur ranks that autumn to play in the European Tour qualifying school. She did, however, appear in one more GB&I Vagliano Trophy team before securing her Tour card by finishing thirteenth in the qualifying school.

There would be no wins in 2004, her first season as a Tour professional, but she did repeat her second place in Tenerife, was third in the Spanish Open and tied third in the KLM Open in Holland. She finished second in the Ryder Cup Wales Rookie of the Year standings and eighth in the Order of Merit.

By most people's standards that would be an impressive start to a career, but Brewerton's standards are on another level altogether.

'If anyone had told me I'd finish eighth on the Order of Merit before the season started, I probably wouldn't have believed them. But looking back there were still some things I was disappointed with. I started the year well but by the time a lot of the big events came along, my form had dipped and I was starting to put too much pressure on myself.'

Brewerton played 16 Tour events in 2005 with three top-ten finishes and was nineteenth on the money list. She also partnered Becky Morgan to finish tied sixth in the World Cup in South Africa.

If the label of being one of the best players on Tour without a win was starting to follow Brewerton, then 2006 was another consistent, but ultimately frustrating, year. Five top-tens in 15 events, and fifteenth on the money list with her highest earnings, was backed up by another impressive World Cup where she and Morgan were tied third at Sun City.

The same pair started 2007 by finishing eighth in the World Cup and then, finally, Brewerton shook the monkey off her back with that emotional win at Chart Hills. She had four other top-ten finishes and her place in the Solheim Cup team was, fittingly, confirmed at the Wales Championship of Europe at Machynys.

Even though she missed the cut in front of her home supporters, Brewerton had done enough to earn a place in Helen Alfredsson's European team to take on the United States at Halmstad, Sweden.

'It was a very nervy weekend at Machynys and it took a while for it to sink in. I was so emotional, I could hardly look at the scores over the final two days. The selection was hanging over me for weeks, so to have it confirmed that I was in the team was such a relief. And to be the first Welsh player to achieve it was amazing and I knew that I'd have the whole nation behind me.'

As the youngest member of the European team at just 24, Brewerton was pitched straight into the heat of battle alongside former world number one Laura Davies, the only player to have appeared in all ten Solheim Cups to that date. They were beaten 2&1 by Juli Inkster and Paula Creamer, and Brewerton then had to wait until the following afternoon for her next taste of the action, when she and Davies defeated Natalie Gulbis and Nicole Castrale by two holes.

As the USA ran riot on the final day to win eight-and-a-half points out of 12 in the singles for a 16-12 overall victory, Brewerton was able to hold her head up high as she fought out a half with twice British Open champion Sherri Steinhauer.

'It was an unbelievable week. Just getting to the course and walking into my room, seeing my golf bag and uniform there was surreal. In the end I couldn't wait for Friday and the competition to start. Until you get there and experience the whole atmosphere it's difficult to describe just how it feels. Plenty of people had told me what to expect, but to be honest it was on a completely different scale to anything I have been through before.

'I was fairly satisfied with my own performances and I played really well against Sherri. A half was probably the worst result I could have got on the day. But obviously I was disappointed with the result overall and that was my motivation to get back into the team for 2009.'

Brewerton's breakthrough year ended with her being named Professional Player of the Year at the Towergate Golf Union of Wales awards.

Another winter's training at her base in Desert Springs, Almeria, was the recipe for what many felt would be an even better year in 2008. But as things materialised 2008 was, in Brewerton's words, 'a boring year' with nine top-ten finishes and fifteenth place on the money list – but no victories.

If 2008 was boring, however, then 2009 was anything but. Seven times in the top-five, Brewerton also chalked up her second Tour victory in the Open de Espana

Feminino, finished third on the money list and retained her place in Europe's Solheim Cup team.

Brewerton was a wild-card pick by European captain Allison Nicholas for the matches at Rich Harvest Farms, Chicago, where the United States prevailed 16-12 . It was a weekend of mixed emotions for the Welsh girl, who partnered Laura Davies to defeat in the opening fourballs, but registered a winning point alongside France's Gwladys Nocera in the foursomes. The same pair gained another point on the second day before Brewerton succumbed 5&4 to Angela Stanford in the singles.

The GUW award for the professional player of the year went to Brewerton for the second time in three years, in the same week she broke into the world's top100 for the first time.

At the age of 27 but with the experience to match many twice her age, Brewerton is set to be the flag-bearer for women's professional golf in Wales for years to come.

'I go into every tournament believing I can win it. That's not arrogance, just common sense as I see it. A lot of the game is about attitude and for me the attitude is to set my goals as high as I possibly can.'

So far most of those goals have been achieved, but Brewerton is not one to rest on her laurels and knows that after her profile reached a new high in 2009 the expectations will be even greater. No doubt the LPGA Tour in America will be on her mind over the next few years, when she will also try to cement a regular place in the European Solheim Cup team and challenge for the Majors.

Brewerton, a natural born winner, really does have the world at her feet.

Brewerton with the trophy after her maiden European Tour win in the English Open at Chart Hills in 2007                                                                 (Ladies' European Tour)

Rhys Davies

## Chapter Twenty
# Rhys Davies

IMAGINE a Welsh singer reaching number one on the Billboard charts in the USA, and you get an idea of the level that Rhys Davies attained in 2007.

The rangy youngster from Bridgend was officially rated number one in the US Collegiate golf rankings in March 2007, the first Welsh player to scale such heights and the first British player to do so since Northern Irishman Graeme McDowell in 2002.

Davies had long since been marked out as one of the bright young things of Welsh, British and European golf, with a CV that had most of the top management agencies in the sport queuing up for his signature when he decided to turn professional.

East Tennessee State University, where Davies spent four years developing his game and studying for a business degree, has rarely seen the like of it. Davies's college career broke record after record, prompting his ETSU coach Fred Warren to nickname him 'The Package.'

'Rhys is an exceptional young man and a talent that you don't come across too often. He's not just a world-class golfer, but a team player and a great leader too. I guess you could refer to him as "The Package."'

Davies, fiercely determined but naturally modest, has played down that description on countless occasions, but Warren was not too far off the mark.

Rhys Davies was born in May 1985 in Bridgend and was educated at Oldcastle Primary School and Brynteg Comprehensive, a real hotbed of sporting talent. Former Welsh rugby skipper (and now coach) Rob Howley, controversial Welsh star Gavin Henson, and cycling's Olympic and World champion Nicole Cooke all passed through the Brynteg ranks ahead of Davies. And it was during these formative years that Davies, whose father Graham is the Director of Performance and Excellence with the Sports Council for Wales, tried his hand at a range of sports.

'I was lucky that I had teachers at Oldcastle who were enthusiastic about sport and I played rugby, football, cricket, tennis and athletics. I first played golf when my father took me along to a nine-hole course in Barry, and it was something I used to do for a weekend treat.'

At the age of eleven, Davies joined Brynhill and then Royal Porthcawl, where his talent was soon spotted by the club's head professional Peter Evans and John Collins, the Glamorgan County junior organiser. However, as his golf progressed, so too did his cricket, and Davies was being moulded by the Glamorgan Academy structure into an all-rounder of some promise, so much so that the England youth selectors were also impressed. Indeed, Davies was part of a set-up which included current Test batsman Alastair Cook.

It wasn't until the age of seventeen that he was finally forced to choose between golf and cricket. The bat and pads were put in the shed and few would argue now that he made the right decision.

'It was a close call and a huge decision for me to have to make. I played for Wales at cricket from under-12 through to under-16 age groups and I would have expected to go on from there to the Glamorgan under-17s and under-19s.'

The decision taken, Davies was already an established Welsh junior golf international and in 2002 he set about making his mark on the bigger stage – something he achieved with a vengeance. He was runner-up in the French Boys' Open Strokeplay early in the year and then, after devoting more time to his sixth-form studies, he reached the semi-finals of the senior Welsh Amateur Championship at Conwy, losing out to the eventual winner David Price.

Davies went straight on to the Boys' Home Internationals at Blairgowrie where he played six matches and won the lot, and then to the Boys' Amateur Championship at Carnoustie. He won six more matches there to reach the final before exhaustion caught up as he was beaten at the 37th hole of a marathon encounter with English youngster Mark Pilling.

'It was a pretty tiring time for me and in the end my short game, and especially my putting, was just off. To get that close to winning such a big event and then falter was a disappointment, but I had to put it behind me because I had a lot more golf to play.'

Davies was named captain of the Great Britain and Ireland Boys' team for the Jacques Leglise Trophy matches against the Continent of Europe in Lausanne. While he was in Switzerland, Davies learned he had been called up from reserve to replace the injured Richard Scott and take his place in the senior Wales team for the Home Internationals at Royal St David's, Harlech. He then played his part in Wales's first success in the quadrangular event in its 70-year history.

'It was a great year but the Home Internationals were the highlight for me. I've always loved playing for Wales and the spirit in the team was something else. Everyone contributed to the overall success and it was so special.'

There was still one more accolade to come for Davies as he was named BBC Wales Junior Sports Personality of the Year.

If the summer of 2002 was busy then twelve months down the line there was no respite for Davies. He reached the final of the Welsh Amateur Championship at Southerndown before losing to Stuart Manley, and then went all the way to the final of the British Boys again, at Royal Liverpool.

Davies had played a staggering 24 competitive rounds of championship golf in the space of 17 days but there was one big difference. This time he claimed a major title. His opponent in the final at Hoylake was the precociously talented Spaniard Pablo Martin-Benavides, who would go on to become a rival to Davies on the collegiate circuit in America and who, in 2007, created history at the Portuguese Open as the first amateur to win a European Tour title.

The memory of losing in the final the previous year spurred Davies on and he edged out Martin to become Wales's first winner of the title for 14 years.

'It was one of those matches that turned out to be pretty scrappy but fiercely contested and I was determined to win after what happened in 2002. It didn't matter how I got across the line, just that I did.'

Another appearance for the GB&I Boys in the Jacques Leglise Trophy signalled the end of Davies's junior career and the start of that remarkable chapter across the Atlantic, where there was no shortage of universities wanting to get Davies on their roster. He chose East Tennessee State, which had a tradition of attracting players from the Celtic nations, notably Irish former Walker Cup star Keith Nolan, who is now assistant coach on the golf programme there.

'It just felt like the right place for me and that's how it turned out. I settled in quickly over there and that certainly helped my golf game.'

Davies's first season Stateside saw him established firmly as number one in the ETSU team and he was named Southern Conference Freshman of the Year. His best tournament finish was second at the Southern Conference Championships and he was also selected for the European Palmer Cup team to face the United States in the student version of the Ryder Cup.

It was in his sophomore year that Davies really hit the headlines, finishing 2004 ranked number three in the States following a remarkable series of results during which his stroke average was better than the one attained by Tiger Woods during his college spell at Stanford University.

Southern Conference Player of the Year, Davies set a new ETSU record in winning five individual titles in one season and secured nine top-three placings in eleven events. There was also a record low score of 63 in the UK Derby Invitational, a record three-round low of 199 in the NCAA East Regionals, and a coveted place in the All American first team.

If that wasn't enough Davies also found time to fly across to Puerto Rico where Wales finished seventh in the World Amateur Championships for the Eisenhower Trophy.

Davies tees off in the NCAA Championship finals, watched by his college coach and mentor Fred Warren

*(ETSU Athletics)*

Davies began his junior (third) year at ETSU in much the same vein, winning the University's host tournament, the Bank of Tennessee Intercollegiate, and tying first in the Shoal Creek Intercollegiate to take his total wins to seven, eclipsing the college record of six previously held by PGA Tour player Garrett Willis.

A Walker Cup debut for GB&I against the United States at Chicago Golf Club in the autumn of 2005 was inevitable, and Davies was duly selected, claiming 2½ points out of four in a narrow 12½-11½ defeat. He proceeded to finish 2005 ranked number three in America and added an eighth individual college title in the spring of 2006 before competing in his second Eisenhower Trophy for Wales in South Africa, where he, Nigel Edwards and Llewellyn Matthews finished fourth.

By then he had also embarked on his senior college year when thoughts of a switch to professional golf were starting to move to the forefront of Davies's mind. Back-to-back wins in the space of two weeks were enough to put the Welshman at number one on Golfweek-Sagarin rankings, a position he already held on the Golfstat.com rankings.

'To attain that number one status and see my name up there was amazing. I just found something in my game that was working and when that happens, you have to make the most of it.'

Davies ended his ETSU career with ten victories, a record that seems likely to stand for many years to come, and the whole college experience was one that seemed to fit him like a golf glove.

'I was doing what I always wanted to do, so that kept me self-motivated. Most people see golf as a very individual sport but in college the team is everything. We all lived in the same apartment, ate meals together, practised together and played tournaments together. I loved the whole time I was there.'

Davies was always going to extend his amateur career to the autumn of 2007 to give himself another crack at the Walker Cup, and his profile was done no harm at all when, in June of that year, he qualified for the US Open Championship at Oakmont. An amateur getting through the notoriously tough qualifiers is something akin to a club tennis player battling through to Wimbledon. But that is exactly what Davies did, shooting rounds of 72 and then 65 at Woodmont, Maryland, to win the sectional qualifier ahead of seasoned Tour winners like Fred Funk and Joey Sindelar.

He missed the cut at Oakmont but took a huge step along the learning curve that will get even steeper in the early stages of his professional career.

'I played a practice round with Masters champion Zach Johnson and he actually congratulated me on my great amateur record. I knew I had a fair amount of publicity in the States but I was really surprised that someone at his level knew about me.

'It was a thrill to play in the US Open but qualifying didn't come as that much of a surprise to me. I was always confident that I could do it and always felt that I could be comfortable competing at that sort of level. That's what I work for and where I want to be. The second day was a bad one for me but the opening round showed me that I can play with these guys on a level field. I asked as many questions as I could of as many people as I could, and they were all really helpful to me.'

There would be no fairy-tale ending to Davies's sensational amateur career, GB&I losing the 2007 Walker Cup at Royal County Down by the same 12½-11½ margin as two years earlier. Davies was twice beaten in foursomes but won both his singles matches during a thrilling weekend on the Northern Irish coast.

Davies immediately turned pro and signed with the global IMG group, but failed to secure either his European or USPGA Tour cards at the first attempt. Undeterred, he spent the final few months of 2007 playing in the early season co-sanctioned European Tour events in Australia and New Zealand, gaining experience of life with the pros week-by-week. For much of 2008 Davies had to rely on the occasional sponsors' invitation to play in the higher profile events as he continued to develop his game wherever he could. But a second trip to Tour School once again came and went without Davies earning himself any playing privileges. In late 2008 and early 2009 he began to make a serious impact on the Asian Tour and then made a major breakthrough closer to home by coming through qualifying at Sunningdale to earn himself a first Open Championship appearance at Turnberry. The week after missing the cut in Scotland, Davies gained his first European Challenge Tour victory on home soil at the Vale of Glamorgan as he landed the Swalec Wales Challenge. A second victory in Spain followed and, finishing fourth on the Challenge Tour rankings, Davies secured his full European Tour card for 2010.

'The main goal for me at the start of the year was to get my European Tour card, and so it was mission accomplished on that score. Now I'm looking forward to having a really good shot at it. The big confidence booster is being able to plan your career for the following twelve months and that is something I haven't been able to do since turning professional. For the three years since joining the paid ranks I was floating between Asia, the Challenge and European tours.

'Now I can focus on doing the best I possibly can on the European Tour for 2010 and that's what I'm really looking forward to.'

His optimism was well founded after a stunning start to the 2010 season which saw a maiden Tour victory in the Hassan Trophy in Morocco followed by a runners-up spot alongside Stephen Dodd – behind USPGA champion Y. E. Yang – in the Volvo China Open.

The Ryder Cup at the Celtic Manor might come a couple of years too early for Davies... but with his track record and undoubted talent, don't rule him out completely.

# Chapter Twenty One

# And the Rest . . .

THERE are, of course, many other fine Welsh golfers whose achievements are worthy of note, stretching back as far as the late Victorian era.

Preceding the dominance of Henry Howell, The Glamorganshire Club at Penarth had already produced a series of Welsh Amateur champions before the onset of the First World War: John Hunter in 1895 and 1896, T.M. Barlow in 1900, James Hunter in 1902 and 1903, John Duncan in 1905 and 1909, and George Renwick in 1906.

Howell excepted, Cardiff's Huw Squirrell is the only player in the post-war era to win the Welsh Amateur three times in succession. Squirrell made the event his own from 1958-1960 and added two more victories in 1964 and 1965.

Llandrindod's John Llewellyn-Morgan won successive championships in 1950 and 1951 and became Wales's first  post-war Walker Cup player in 1951. He also represented Great Britain and Ireland against the USA in 1953 and 1955, a record that stood until Nigel Edwards made a fourth appearance in the event in 2007.

Radyr's Jeff Toye was Welsh champion in 1969 and again in 1975, and went on to serve Wales and GB&I as a captain and selector.

Langland Bay's John Roger Jones won back-to-back titles in 1983 and 1984, and has also been an influential member of both the Welsh Golfing Union and the Royal and Ancient.

Albert Evans, winner of the Welsh Amateur in 1949 and again in 1961 out of the Brecon club, played for Wales in the very first Home Internationals in 1932 and made his final appearance in 1961. He reached the semi-finals of the Amateur Championship at Royal Porthcawl in 1951 where defeat by the American Charlie Coe denied him the opportunity to become only Wales's second finalist after Tony Duncan. Evans also captained Wales with distinction, and went on to become one of the game's foremost administrators, serving as Chairman of the Welsh Golfing Union from 1972-1978 and President from 1979-1983. After Tony Duncan, he was only the second Honorary Member of the Union.

Rhos-on-Sea's Jimmy Buckley completed the double of Welsh matchplay and strokeplay titles in 1968 and played in the 1979 GB&I Walker Cup team.

Duncan Evans became Wales's first British Amateur champion at Royal Porthcawl in 1980 and played in the following year's Walker Cup.

Clyne's Neil Roderick, a Welsh strokeplay champion, attained Walker Cup honours in 1989 as did David Park (1997) and Stuart Manley (2003).

Former Walker Cup player and European Tour winner David Park          *(Media Wales)*

Park, a product of the Burghill Valley club in Herefordshire, won the Brabazon Trophy (The English Amateur Open Strokeplay) ahead of Sergio Garcia and Geoff Ogilvy, before turning pro after his Walker Cup debut. In his first event on the full European Tour in 1999, Park was denied victory by Miguel Angel Martin at the sixth extra hole of a sudden death play-off in the Moroccan Open. A week later he was not to be denied, winning the European Grand Prix at Slaley Hall by a stroke from David Carter and Retief Goosen.

Manley, from Mountain Ash, was Welsh champion in 2003 before embarking on his European Tour career.

Southerndown's Llewellyn Matthews, who appeared in the 2007 Walker Cup at Royal County Down before turning professional, was the 2006 and 2007 Welsh champion and also achieved the distinction of qualifying for the 2007 Open Championship at Carnoustie as an amateur. Matthews also won the prestigious St Andrews Links Trophy with a record low aggregate.

Maesdu's Clive Brown, Welsh champion in 1971, never reached Walker Cup heights as a player, but did so as Great Britain and Ireland's non-playing captain in 1995 and 1997. And he will forever be associated with the winning 1995 team at Royal Porthcawl as they defeated the United States, Tiger Woods and all.

The name of Bert Hodson may not be familiar to many but the Newport-born player actually became Wales's first Ryder Cup golfer when he played in the beaten GB&I team in Ohio in 1931. He lost his only match against Densmore (Denny) Shute, who would go on to win The Open Championship two years later and two USPGA titles. Assistant professional at the Newport golf club, Hodson later moved to Chigwell in Essex where he became head pro and a mentor to Michael Bonallack, who won five Amateur championships and, as secretary of the R&A, was knighted for his services to golf.

David Llewellyn enjoyed a European Tour career that spanned 20 years from 1971-1991, and also enjoyed successful spells as a club professional and as National Coach to the Welsh Golfing Union. He will always be remembered, however, for his 1987 World Cup of Golf victory in Hawaii alongside Ian Woosnam. Llewellyn holed the winning putt to secure Wales's first success in the event. His only European Tour win came in the 1988 Biarritz Open, where a bogey on the final hole during a third round 60 cost him the chance to become the first player in Tour history to register a magical 59.

Llewellyn also enjoyed considerable success on the African Tour, including a victory in the 1991 Ivory Coast Open.

St Athan-born Mark Mouland can claim to be one of the European Tour's genuine stalwarts, starting his professional career as a 20-year-old in 1981 and plying his trade on the main and Challenge Tours ever since. A British Boys' champion in 1976, Mouland followed in the footsteps of his father Sid, who was a dominant figure on the Welsh professional scene in the 1960s and won the Welsh PGA Championship no fewer than six times.

Mouland junior won his first Tour title at Moortown, Leeds, in the 1986 Care Plan International, finishing a shot ahead of Sweden's Anders Forsbrand.

After recovering from a horrific car accident, Mouland added a second title in the 1988 KLM Dutch Open at Hilversum. He also claimed successive Mauritius Open titles on the Challenge Tour in 2002 and 2003, and represented Wales in seven Dunhill Cups and eight World Cups.

Cardiff's Richard Johnson, the son of one of Wales's most respected teaching professionals Peter Johnson, secured a PGA Tour card in the United States for 2008 after topping the Nationwide Tour Order of Merit in 2007. A member of Wales's victorious side in the 1993 European Amateur Team Championship in the Czech Republic, he made his home in the United States after graduating from Augusta State University in 1995.

In 2007 he enjoyed a breakthrough year with victories in the Mark Christopher Charity Classic and the season-ending Nationwide Tour Championship in California, which clinched him top spot on the Order of Merit and the chance to rub shoulders with the big guns of the main Tour in 2008.

Wales also had a European Challenge Tour Order of Merit winner in 2006 as Nefyn's Mark Pilkington, the 1998 Welsh Amateur champion, topped the money list and recorded a victory in the Kazakhstan Open.

Church Village born Jamie Donaldson, who helped Great Britain and Ireland's Amateur team to second place in the World Championships for the Eisenhower Trophy in 2000, has gone on to emerge as a rising force on the European Tour and partnered Stephen Dodd for his World Cup of Golf debut in China in 2009.

And looking to the future, 2009 saw Wales select their youngest ever player in the team for the amateur Home Internationals with Rhys Pugh, from the Vale of Glamorgan club, representing his country at Hillside, Lancashire, still a month shy of his sixteenth birthday.

In the women's game Blanche Duncan was the first multiple Welsh title holder, winning the Welsh Ladies' Championship four times in succession from 1906-1909 and for a fifth time in 1912. And the Duncan dynasty continued with Margery Duncan's three titles in 1922, 1927 and 1928.

Margaret Cox claimed three successive Welsh titles from 1923-1925, whilst Mary Jestyn Jeffreys also completed a hat-trick in 1930, 1931 and 1933.

Former Curtis Cup international and Ladies' European Tour player Helen Wadsworth

*(Media Wales)*

The great Nancy Wright (nee Cook), was the player to beat in the 1950s, winning the Welsh Championship in 1953, 1954, 1955 and 1958. She went on to add two more in 1965 and 1967. Her record of six titles stood until Vicki Thomas won her seventh of eight in 1991.

Mary Oliver won three Welsh titles in the 1960s and Audrey Briggs four in the 1970s before the Thomas era began.

Helen Wadsworth, winner of the Welsh Women's Open Strokeplay title in 1986, achieved Curtis Cup honours in 1990, becoming only the third Welsh player (after Tegwen Perkins and Thomas) to be named in the GB&I team.

Royal Liverpool's Lisa Dermott earned Curtis Cup colours in 1996, the year she won her second successive Welsh title.

And Sarah Jones, a product of the Pennard club where Thomas enjoyed so many glorious years, appeared in the 2002 Curtis Cup side and went on to win Welsh Championships back-to-back in 2004 and 2005.

Anna Highgate (2004) and Breanne Loucks (2006 and 2008) are the latest Welsh women to appear in the Curtis Cup, Wrexham's Loucks also adding the Welsh title in 2007.

Not a bad cast list for such a small nation . . .

# Dragons
## and Fairways